FRIEDRICH HEBBEL

TWAYNE'S WORLD AUTHORS SERIES

A Survey of the World's Literature

Sylvia E. Bowman, Indiana University

GENERAL EDITOR

GERMANY

Ulrich Weisstein, Indiana University

EDITOR

Friedrich Hebbel

(TWAS 56)

TWAYNE'S WORLD AUTHORS SERIES (TWAS)

*The purpose of TWAS is to survey the major writers
—novelists, dramatists, historians, poets, philosophers,
and critics—of the nations of the world. Among the
national literatures covered are those of Australia,
Canada, China, Eastern Europe, France, Germany,
Greece, India, Italy, Japan, Latin America, New Zea-
land, Poland, Russia, Scandinavia, Spain, and the
African nations, as well as Hebrew, Yiddish, and
Latin Classical literatures. This survey is comple-
mented by Twayne's United States Authors Series
and English Authors Series*

*The intent of each volume in these series is to present
a critical-analytical study of the works of the writer;
to include biographical and historical material that
may be necessary for understanding, appreciation,
and critical appraisal of the writer; and to present all
material in clear, concise English—but not to vitiate
the scholarly content of the work by doing so.*

Friedrich Hebbel

By **STEN G. FLYGT**

Vanderbilt University

Twayne Publishers, Inc.   ::   New York

Preface

This book is an attempt to introduce its readers to the work and personality of one of the most remarkable German dramatists since Schiller. For this reason, notes and scholarly paraphernalia have been kept to a minimum and learned controversy has been avoided. The book does not seek to "prove" anything, but rather to present its subject in such a way as to contribute to a more general understanding of a significant, if not exactly lovable writer, who has enriched world literature with two or three compelling dramas.

I am particularly pleased to acknowledge my indebtedness to Vanderbilt University for making time available to complete this study.

All translations from the German are my own.

STEN G. FLYGT

Vanderbilt University
Nashville, Tennessee

Contents

FRIEDRICH HEBBEL

by
STEN G. FLYGT

This volume is a comprehensive literary criticism and analysis of the works of Friedrich Hebbel, nineteenth-century German playwright and poet, who has been identified outside the German-speaking world as one of the fore-runners of the still more famous Nor-wegian dramatist, Henrik Ibsen. Hebbel brought at least two things of great importance to the German theater: penetrating and analytical revelation of the motives of his characters, and a con-ception of historical determinism, as can be seen, for example, in his *Herodes und Mariamne*.

Professor Flygt presents Friedrich Hebbel in such a way that he can be seen as a figure of stature and indepen-dence, rather than as merely a connect-ing link in the history of European drama. Extensive biographical material and a chronology of Hebbel's life are also included.

Chronology

1813 Born in Wesselburen.

1827 Death of father; employed by Mohr.

1828 Early literary efforts; association with congenial group of amateurs; self-education in Mohr's library.

1832 Insight into nature of poetry from reading Uhland; first letter from Amalie Schoppe.

1833 Composition of "Die Schlacht bei Hemmingstedt."

1834 Poems in nature-mystical vein; arrangements for study in Hamburg completed by Dr. Schoppe.

1835 Move to Hamburg and beginning of formal studies; diaries begun; acquaintance with Elise Lensing.

1836 Study of jurisprudence in Heidelberg—soon abandoned; acquaintance with Emil Rousseau; move to Munich; some novellas and poems written; acquaintance with Josefa Schwarz; composition of stories, "Schnock" and "Der Schneidermeister Nepomuk Schlägel auf der Freudenjagd."

1837 Composition of lyric poems.

1838 Death of mother; death of Emil Rousseau.

1839 Return to Hamburg on foot; resumption of (stormy) relations with Amalie Schoppe.

1840 *Judith* completed January 27, performed in Berlin July 13; acquaintance with Emma Schröder; son Max born November 5.

1841 *Genoveva* completed March 1, published July 4; *Der Diamant* completed November 29.

1842 First audience with King Christian VIII.

1843 Travel stipend received April 12; "Mein Wort über das Drama" published July 31; residence in Paris; death of Max October 2; *Maria Magdalene* finished December 4.

1844 Second son, Ernst, born May 14; *Maria Magdalene* published; travel in Italy.

1845 Work on *Moloch* and *Julia;* acquaintance with Christine Enghaus, the turning point in Hebbel's life, December 24.

1846 Marriage to Christine Enghaus, May 26; birth of third son, Emil, December 27.

1847 Completion of *Ein Trauerspiel in Sizilien;* death of Emil February 14; death of Ernst May 12; *Der Diamant* published; visit of Elise Lensing in Vienna May 29, 1847-August 27, 1848; trips to Graz and Berlin; *Julia* completed October 23; birth of Christine (Titi) Hebbel, December 25.

1848 *Maria Magdalene* performed in Vienna May 8; member of writers' delegation to Emperor in Innsbruck May 26-June 8; *Herodes und Mariamne* completed November 14.

1849 *Herodes und Mariamne* performed in Vienna April 19; *Der Rubin* completed May 19; first act of *Moloch* completed June 12; acquaintance with Emil Kuh.

1850 *Herodes und Mariamne* published January; visit with Christine to Hamburg and renewal of friendship with Elise; *Der Rubin* published October 8; *Moloch,* second act, completed October 25; *Michel Angelo* finished December 18.

1851 Travels to Berlin and Hamburg; *Epilog* of *Genoveva* completed January 21; *Agnes Bernauer* finished December 14.

1852 Travels to Munich, Venice, Milan; *Agnes Bernauer* performed in Munich April 25; presentation to royalty.

1853 Travels to Hamburg and Helgoland.

1854 Travels to Marienbad and Prague; completion of *Gyges und sein Ring* November 14; death of Elise November 18.

1855 Purchase of house in Gmunden on the Traunsee.

1856 The epic poem, *Mutter und Kind,* begun.

1857 Travels to Hamburg, Frankfurt, Weimar, Stuttgart; completion of *Siegfrieds Tod* February 18; completion of *Mutter und Kind* March 20; publication of *Collected Poems* September; Tiedge Prize awarded for *Mutter und Kind; Demetrius* begun.

1858 Completion of *Der Steinwurf,* opera libretto commissioned by Anton Rubinstein, March 16; presentation to Grand Duke Karl Alexander of Sachsen-Weimar; travels to Weimar, Krakau; *Mutter und Kind* published at Christmas.

Chronology

1859 Work on *Die Nibelungen* resumed.

1860 Break with Emil Kuh, end of January; completion of *Die Nibelungen;* trip to Paris.

1861 Performance of *Die Nibelungen* I and II in Weimar, January 31; performance of entire work in Weimar May 16 and 18; thoughts of moving to Weimar given up after October.

1862 Travels to Paris, London; guest of Grand Duke Karl Alexander in Wilhelmstal in mid-August.

1863 Performance of *Die Nibelungen* I and II in Vienna; beginning of fatal illness, March 16; appointed Private Librarian to the Grand Duke of Weimar, March 18; various public honors; work on *Demetrius* resumed in October; awarded the Schiller Prize November 7; death December 13.

CHAPTER 1

The Beginnings

I *Boyhood*

A PERSON who is describing his own life should, like Goethe, emphasize only the enjoyable, beautiful, comforting, and compensating elements which can be found even in the gloomiest situation, and let the other things take care of themselves." So runs a rather remarkable self-admonition from the pen of the young Christian Friedrich Hebbel, whose early years were filled with gloom of the deepest sort. The autobiography which he set out to write at the age of twenty-nine was never completed, but he did get far enough with it in subsequent fits of writing to provide us with an idyllic picture of extreme poverty, the only idyll he ever wrote except for the little-known but very impressive *Mutter und Kind*.

The first six of Hebbel's fourteen childhood years were at least not intolerable. His parents, Klaus Friedrich and Antje Margarete (Schubart), "owned" the house of which they occupied a part. The quotation marks are appropriate because the father, a rather inept bricklayer and repairman, had guaranteed a loan for a friend who had been unable to meet his obligations. The Hebbel family was therefore merely tolerated in the house which they called theirs until such time as the creditor was released from prison and able to evict them. But still the garden was there for the boy's pleasure, and he was wealthy in the sight of his playmates when the pear tree bore its fruit. More important than the purposeful adulation of his contemporaries was, if we can trust the adult Hebbel's reminiscences, the benevolence of the older people who made up his world. There was, for instance, Klaus Ohl, the bankrupt builder, whose cheerful nature had not been affected by adversity, and who took no real joy in the simple pleasures still open to him unless the children could share in them. Even Ohl's wife, who did not share her husband's happy disposition, was kind to the children, and read them stories from the Bible, notably the terrible passage in which Jeremiah prophesies that in the time of extreme need the mothers will slaughter their own children and eat them. "I still remember the sense of horror this passage produced in me, perhaps because I did not know whether it referred to the past or the future, to Jerusalem or Wesselburen [Hebbel's native town], and because I was a child myself and had a mother."

The little boy's sense of the gruesome and the terrible was heightened by the tales of witches and ghosts that he heard from the old storyteller, Meta, whose brazen features reminded him of Old Testament characters. In the dusk of winter evenings, the children would gather around her and hear tales of the Blocksberg and the Witches' Sabbath, and of the wicked miller's wife, who changed herself into a cat every night until the miller's apprentice cut off a paw, as a result of which she bled to death from the loss of her hand. But the most important inhabitant of the child's world was his kind and loving mother, who would have been indulgent if the means at her disposal had only permitted. On some occasions she did try to see that her children received some extra tidbit, but such an attempt was likely to end in disaster, for Klaus Friedrich was compelled by circumstances to play the role of domestic tyrant and enforce a program of austerity in all respects. Later, after he had had to give up his property, he became utterly embittered.

In his fourth year, Christian Friedrich was sent to a pre-elementary school taught by a pipe-smoking old maid named Susanna. Susanna managed her pupils by a system of punishments and rewards. On her desk lay a ruler with which to rap the knuckles of the unruly pupils and a bag of raisins for the delectation of those considered worthy. In this school the boy learned to read but not to write, for writing was a mystery which Susanna explained only to the oldest pupils since her own fund of skills and knowledge encompassed nothing more. Young Christian did, however, learn something else in Susanna's school, namely, a practical illustration of the Gospel truth, "Unto everyone that hath shall be given." On all occasions, but especially at Christmas time, Susanna was very partial in her gift-giving. The daughters of the parish-clerk, the sons of the physician, and the children of prosperous parents received cookies, nuts, and other goodies. The children of the poor did not fare so well. Here, of course, it was the law of reciprocity that was operative. Little Christian was somewhat better off than the other poor children because Susanna received some of the fruit of the productive pear tree mentioned earlier. Nonetheless, he did become aware of the discrimination, and to a large extent because Susanna's maid taunted him with his presumed beggary. "As soon as Susanna's partiality and her maid's injustice penetrated to my consciousness," he wrote later, "I had stepped out of the magic circle of childhood. This happened very early."

Great changes took place in Christian Friedrich's life in his sixth year, when an elementary school was built in the little town of Wesselburen in Norderdithmarschen, where he lived. (Parenthetically, it should be pointed out that Dithmarschen was part of the Duchy of Holstein, the sovereign of which was also King of Denmark). The establishment of this school brought a new and better qualified teacher to Wesselburen, Franz Christian Dethlefsen, whose name Hebbel could not write down without a feeling of deepest gratitude. But at the time that he exchanged Susanna's musty schoolroom for the bright and cheerful elementary school, his father was called upon to surrender his modest home and garden and move into much less adequate quarters. In the general estimation, the Hebbels sank very low on the scale of social prestige because of this misfortune. The boy's old playmates cut themselves off from him or, at the least, caused him to smart for the loss in status, for now there was only one class lower than his own, that of the orphans, who were supported by public funds. But, perhaps there were some good consequences, for if the boy had hitherto been a soft and gentle dreamer, he was now thrust into the struggle of life and was forced to defend himself with his fists. If he dreaded and tried to avoid the first such violent encounter, he feared the second one less and found the third quite pleasurable. The bellicosity which he presumably acquired in this way never forsook him.

The altered circumstances of the family intensified the grinding poverty which the boy had experienced less keenly during his first four years. The loss of the house which he had inherited from his family, and the despairing knowledge that he could never still the hunger of his children, produced in Klaus Friedrich an actual hatred of Christian and his younger brother Johann. They were his wolves to whom he was inseparably chained and who almost literally snatched the bread from his lips. Still, so Hebbel was convinced in later life, Klaus Friedrich was a good and well-intentioned man but poverty had taken the place of his heart. Only at Christmas time did he relax his severity and permit his family to taste the joys of the season. Then they had a pudding with raisins or plums, perhaps, and good tea. Before the meal, the father and his two sons sang a hymn, and afterwards young Christian had to read aloud the appropriate Gospel passages and a sermon. For two days everyone was permitted to be cheerful and even to laugh and joke a bit, but then the normal atmosphere of worry and bitterness returned.

If only by contrast, school must have been a blessed escape; but to little Christian it was more than that, for Rector Dethlefsen, who realized that the boy had unusual abilities, encouraged him to read and instilled in him respect for language. Not only that, he also helped to pay for the candles which Christian needed to read by in the long winter evenings, an occupation which only vexed the father, who felt that his son's trifling with poetry, drawing, and music could only distract him from pursuits which would help him to earn a living. Accordingly, even though it was plain that the occupation of bricklayer or hod carrier in Wesselburen had little promise, Klaus Friedrich determined to force his son to follow in his footsteps. After a while, it was not possible to doubt that the boy had no talent for bricklaying whatsoever, for he seemed to get more mortar on himself than on the bricks, and the father lost all hope that his son would ever amount to anything.

For the next two years Christian Friedrich tried one petty occupation after another. He ran errands, he helped the local postman, and he continued to read whatever he could lay his hands on. When he was fourteen years old, his father died and was buried in a coffin which was obtained through barter for some of the winter's supply of potatoes. The widow Hebbel worked as a domestic in various homes, but what she brought in was pitifully inadequate. Help was needed from without if the family was not to face starvation.

II *Escape*

Providentially, as it would seem, soon after the father's death help did come and lightened the burden resting upon the widow's shoulders. Christian Friedrich was given food and lodging, in return for various services, in the house of J. J. Mohr, whose title of *Kirchspielvogt* can be roughly translated as parish magistrate. In the course of the nearly eight years that he worked for Mohr, he advanced to the position of parish clerk, or *Kirchspielschreiber,* and had so far won Mohr's confidence that he might at times serve as the magistrate's deputy, an office of considerable eminence for a young man of such lowly origin.

Just how the boy Hebbel came to enter Mohr's service is uncertain. Emil Kuh, who knew Hebbel intimately, gives the more or less official version in his biography. According to this, Christian Friedrich had had occasion to perform menial services for Mohr's household. One day a certain Kirchspielvogt Boijsen, visiting his colleague Mohr, noticed the handsome lad and observed that Mohr might make better use of him. This, along with Rector Dethlefsen's praise for young Hebbel, induced Mohr to offer him the post mentioned above. The implication of this account is that Mohr was exploiting the boy.

As the years passed, it is likely that Mohr divested himself of an increasing number of responsibilities he found irksome, especially since the youthful Hebbel enjoyed the prestige and power lent him by his authority to issue visas and perform other police duties. But it would probably be a mistake to imagine the parish magistrate taking his ease while the parish clerk toiled unrecognized and unrewarded. The fact seems to have been that the duties of this office were so light that both magistrate and clerk were far from being overburdened. According to the poet Klaus Groth, six years younger than Hebbel and also a native of Dithmarschen, clerical posts such as Hebbel's were sought for sons of prosperous citizens because they frequently led to responsible office and entailed very little work. It therefore seems likely that Mohr had no real interest in employing the boy, and that in doing so he yielded, as his son Otto Mohr maintained, to the importunities of Hebbel's kin (no doubt primarily the well-nigh desperate mother) and of Rector Dethlefsen. Moreover, when we consider Otto Mohr's statement that his father had no need of an errand-boy, and that the clerkship required only two or three hours of attention per day, Mohr's employment of Hebbel begins to look like an act of benevolence, the first of a long series which aided Hebbel in his bitter struggle to gain social and literary recognition.[1]

To the youngster, who looked back on fourteen years of poverty and repression, this change in his fortunes must have seemed like an entry into Paradise. He took his meals with the servants, and at this time could scarcely have considered himself anything but another servant. His mealtimes were regular with abundant food, and there is no record of his having to leave the table hungry. Neither is there any record of his having to suffer from the cold in the wintertime, as there was plenty of fuel in Mohr's house. And if the boy had to share a bed with Christoph Sievers, the coachman, this was in no way an exceptional practice, and Sievers, whose mental capacity far exceeded that of the ordinary coachman, became his good friend. Mohr's son, commenting on Hebbel's later abuse of his father, points out that it was the custom of the country for the clerk to be counted among the servants, and that he, Otto Mohr himself, as a grown young man had to share a bed with his brother.

It was only later, in retrospect, that Hebbel saw his years in Mohr's house as a hell. As he grew into manhood he felt out of place, hampered and held back in every way from pursuing a career that would bring him eminence. But at the outset he rather admired Mohr, and so imitated his gait and gestures that they became and remained his own until the day of his death. Mohr's influence upon him extended beyond these mere externals to become a component of his mentality and will, a habit of mind which the poet later said he had learned from Mohr. And that came about when Hebbel, talking boastfully to some friends, was asked to find a certain document for Mohr. When he could not find it in a confused pile of papers, Mohr, without saying a word, separated the official documents from Hebbel's private writings, classified the documents by date and number, and left with the item he wanted. Hebbel was so profoundly embarrassed, he himself admitted, that he became an extreme

[18]

pedant from that instant, unable to tolerate carelessness and lack of order. The change in Hebbel's conduct of his office did not escape Mohr: when Hebbel left Wesselburen to acquire knowledge and pursue fame, Mohr recommended him for his accuracy, industry, and orderliness, praised him for contributing to the support of his mother, and expressed his belief that the young man had an aptitude for business.

Mohr, however, had not treated young Hebbel as the genius he felt himself to be, and maintained the distinction which lay in the nature of their relation as employer and employee, that of upper class to lower class. It is also likely that Mohr felt himself repelled by Hebbel's personality, for Christian Friedrich was at this time already overbearing and arrogant, and he was still crude and boorish. Despite what was probably a considerable antipathy, however, Mohr allowed Hebbel the use of his library, which contained over a thousand volumes, not merely professional books, but also numerous general works, the German classics, and translations from French and English. It was here that Hebbel laid the foundation of the very imposing intellectual structure which he was able to erect in his lifetime. Without this library the furnishings of Hebbel's mind would have been very different, a fact which he did not like to acknowledge even to himself, for he hated to be beholden to anyone for anything, especially for ideas which he claimed as his own. One might suppose that Hebbel would have had, if not a warm sense of obligation, at least a certain feeling of gratitude, however cool. And it seems that while he was still in Wesselburen, although trying to get away, he actually did have such a feeling.

In a letter to Ludwig Uhland, dated August 8, 1832, in which he implores Uhland to help him embark on a literary career, he writes: "Immediately after my father's death, I was taken into the house of Kirchspielvogt Mohr, a man who is as philanthropical as he is cultivated, in order to assist him in many tasks. My employer treats me as well as I can possibly wish. I could therefore very well be content with my situation. However, there is almost no opportunity here for me to acquire some education, which I would like so very much to acquire. My employer understands this himself and has said to me on various occasions that I am not in the right place. But he did not know of a way out any more than I did."[2] Even as late as October,

1834, Hebbel had apparently not come to hate his employer, for in that month and on his own initiative, he composed a complimentary poem on the occasion of Mohr's wedding. Two years later, however, when he was a student at Heidelberg, in a letter to Elise Lensing (August 20, 1836) he complained of his lack of social graces, attributing his awkwardness to Mohr, whom he intended to thank for it in a fitting way. Six years later he wrote in his diary (January 14, 1842): "Where else does my shy, embarrassed manner come from except from the circumstance that this person not only cut me off from every opportunity to learn social behavior at the age when it must be acquired, but also from the circumstance that by compelling me to eat at the same table with coachman and stablemaid he humiliated me profoundly. I will never get over this, and for that reason I do not have the right to forgive it."

From this and other evidence it begins to look as though Hebbel's hatred of Mohr did not arise in him as long as he was in Wesselburen, even though he felt thoroughly out of place there. If his position as Mohr's clerk had been intolerable, it would not have been difficult for him, with his amply attested knowledge and ability, to find a clerkship elsewhere. But, to judge by the tone of his letters to various friends, he had the *joie de vivre* which is normal for that age, and apparently did not see Mohr as a pestilential plant-louse creeping over his vigorous youth, as he once wrote to Elise Lensing (December 14, 1836). This view of his boyhood and early manhood seems in a way to be the reverse of the idyllic view of his childhood which we have already noted, and it seems not implausible that both views were produced by identical impulses to correct the truth, impulses which had their origin in, or at least were similar to, his creative urges. Be that as it may, on many other occasions Hebbel rearranged the facts of circumstances or episodes of his life to make the impression he preferred.

If we consider Hebbel's hatred of Mohr in this light, it begins to seem at least possible, and very likely probable, that the most grievous of the charges he made against Mohr was fictitious. This was made in a letter to Mohr, dated July 15, 1854. The occasion was Mohr's refusal to be one of the contributors to a collection of essays on Hebbel which Emil Kuh was planning to publish. In his letter of refusal, Mohr showed very plainly that he was not impressed by Hebbel's attainments and that he continued to regard him *de haut en bas*. Hebbel, in one of his so-called berserker rages—his admirers frequently referred to him as a Viking—carefully copied some fifteen hundred words of a letter of icy abuse into his diary for the benefit of future biographers. The original he sent to Mohr, who refused to accept it. The climax of the letter is the accusation that Mohr tried to induce Hebbel to marry a servant whom Mohr had gotten pregnant. The accusation is accompanied by Hebbel's threat to expose Mohr in his memoirs unless he formally declared to Emil Kuh that he disavowed the views expressed in his refusal to contribute to the book of essays.

As has been said, the accusation may very well not be true: the only reference to the matter is in this copied portion of the letter; surely Hebbel would have written about it somewhere else, in connection with the man whom he likened to a plant-louse sucking out his vitality.[3] One is inclined to assume this viewpoint when one recalls a passage in the diaries for January 5, 1836: "There are acts of injustice which only one particular person can commit against another one and the magnitude of which the injured person can reveal only by committing an equal number against the other. This is the relationship in which I find myself to Kirchspielvogt Mohr in Wesselburen."

Even though Hebbel was compelled to eat at the servants' table in Mohr's house, he sought and found companionship elsewhere. There were a good many young men in Wesselburen and the nearby town of Heide who had intellectual and esthetic interests, and Hebbel became the center and leader of such a circle. In the winter of 1831-32, he made an attempt to take part in amateur theatricals, but was eventually convinced that as an actor he was quite untalented. For the most part, however, entertainment was furnished by conversation and flirtation. The friends would meet for conversation Sunday afternoons at the house of the builder, Paul Elvers, with whose daughter, Wiebke, Hebbel carried on a flirtation. At the same time he felt a deeper attraction to Emilie Voss, daughter of Kirchspielschreiber Voss, for whom he cherished a feeling of real affection all his life. Being simultaneously attracted to or involved with two women was a recurring experience with Hebbel, one which contributed its own poignancy to the pangs of conscience he suffered for the wrong which he believed to be a metaphysical necessity inherent in the relation between the sexes. One may even wonder whether Hebbel's belief in metaphysical guilt may not have been a subconscious device to lessen the crushing weight of personal guilt resting upon his shoulders. Be that as it may, the problem of guilt, personal and tragic, became in the course of time central to his plays.

Playwriting, however, was not the form which Christian Friedrich's earliest attempts at literary expression took. Poems and short stories seem to be the natural forms for budding writers, and Hebbel was no exception in this respect. He began at fifteen or sixteen to write some occasional verse and derivative poems which show the influence of Schiller. The discovery of a poem by Ludwig Uhland was of great moment to him. Here he learned that what he had considered the mark of true poetry, reflection and generalization, was in fact unpoetic, and that the poet's task was to present the universal through the particular. His own efforts, however, even after reading Uhland, are in the wild romantic vein of E.T.A. Hoffman, fructified by ideas drawn from the nature mysticism of Gotthilf Heinrich Schubert, which the young Hebbel read with desperate seriousness in order to evolve his own view of the world. Since Schubert was greatly influenced by Schelling, Hebbel became familiar with many of the philosopher's leading ideas even before he read Schelling himself, just as he became acquainted with some of Hegel's ideas through intensive study of Feuerbach, whose early idealistic naturalism supported and supplemented the intellectual structure which Hebbel had begun to erect with an intensity and speed that arouses astonishment.

Later in his life (September 15, 1852) in an autobiographical letter to Arnold Ruge, Hebbel was able to say with some justification that, since leaving Wesselburen at the age of twenty-two, he had not gotten any really new idea. He did not, however, either in this letter or anywhere else, ever acknowledge his indebtedness to any of the thinkers mentioned, preferring everyone to believe that he had independently hit upon the very ideas which they had evolved. As Wolfgang Liepe has said, Hebbel regarded Schubert's nature-mysticism as his private body of secret knowledge, by means of which he asserted and maintained his superiority over his associates and which pride would not permit him to acknowledge as having been acquired from anyone.[4]

As Hebbel grew older, and as he gained experience and knowledge, the sense of being misplaced and confined grew increasingly, and it became his great urge to widen his horizons. In 1832, when he was nineteen, he began to make more determined efforts to establish contact with the outside world. When his conception of poetry was revolutionized by the reading of Uhland's "Des Sängers Fluch," he wrote to Uhland, imploring him for help in finding some kind of employment in Stuttgart which would allow him to further his education. Uhland's reply, which was very kind, expressed the poet's regret that he had no possibility of acceding to this request. Hebbel then recalled that he was a Danish subject and wrote to the famous Danish poet and playwright Adam Oehlenschläger, petitioning him to induce the king to grant him some sort of stipend. This venture was also without success. But another effort to establish contact with the outside world fared somewhat better. Hebbel's earlier attempts at literary expression had appeared in the local *Dithmarser und Eiderstedter Bote,* but now he sent some poems and stories full of local patriotism to a journal in Hamburg, the *Pariser Modeblätter,* edited by Amalie Schoppe, one of the most profilic writers of her day, now deservedly forgotten.

This proved to be the fateful step which led to the first decisive turning point in Hebbel's life. Amalie Schoppe, who had known prosperity and adversity and who had made a kind of place for herself in the literary world by dint of her own energy and determination, fancied herself in the role of patroness of budding authors. She not only accepted Hebbel's contributions but encouraged him to send her more and he, of course, asked for her help to get out of Wesselburen. Although she was unable to help him at this time, she continued to write him letters of sound advice until, early in 1834, she told him that she might be able to find a position for him in a stationer's shop that was operated in connection with a lottery. She, therefore, urged him to write a letter of application for this position, which would give him plenty of time to pursue his studies. She told him exactly what to say in the letter and instructed him to send it, unsealed, to her, so that she could determine whether it would have the right effect. Nothing came of this effort either, but in July, 1834, Amalie wrote that her efforts on Hebbel's behalf had finally borne fruit. She had persuaded a number of friends and acquaintances to enable him to realize his ambitions: they had undertaken to provide him with some money and free board in the homes of his benefactors.

The door to fame and glory stood slightly ajar, and Hebbel prepared to slip through.

CHAPTER 2

A Larger World

I Hamburg and Heidelberg

THE preparations which both Hebbel and Amalie Schoppe had to make took a few months, but finally, toward the end of February, 1835, he set out for Hamburg, accompanied part of the way by some of his friends. After reaching Hamburg and moving into a room rented for him by Amalie Schoppe, he presented himself to the various benefactors who had undertaken to support him, no doubt a galling task to anyone as fiercely independent as Hebbel. Even more galling was the arrangement, also made by Amalie Schoppe, of being a non-paying boarder at the table of certain of the benefactors. Dr. Schoppe had already instructed her protégé that the recipient of such benefactions was to make himself as inconspicuous as possible and disappear immediately after the repast. She had also instructed him that the acquisition of certain social graces would be very helpful to him in making his way. Here, of course, she touched Hebbel's sore point: in this one respect he had a sense of inferiority and a dread that his deficiency might forever keep him from attaining the distinction which he craved.

In respect to his poetic genius and to the force and depth of his thought, Hebbel never acknowledged any save the greatest superiors: Shakespeare, Goethe, Kant. In the autobiographical letter to Arnold Ruge of September 15, 1852, looking back upon his first weeks in Hamburg, he writes, "Since my twenty-second year, when I began to lead the intellectual life and made up for the omissions of the past, I have not acquired a single really new idea." And it is possible that in a certain sense this assertion was true. At any rate, when, on March 23, 1835, he began to record his "Reflections on the World, Life, and Books, but Especially on Myself in the Form of a Diary," he wrote, with a kind of wry irony which only half-concealed earnest conviction, that he intended his journal to be not only a notebook of his heart, but also an aid to his future biographer; for his chance of attaining immortality was certain. Here he meant not only that he hoped for fame in the ordinary literary sense, but also that he felt himself to be a true poet, one who reveals the meaning of the world and the nature of God. And here it should be stated incidentally that the journal which he began at this time constitutes one of his most valid claims to immortality, for, as the repository of his inmost thoughts, it is a most remarkable book of confessions coupled with philosophical speculations in aphoristic form.

All things considered, it probably was not long before Hebbel felt sorely disappointed with his new circumstances in Hamburg, where his intellectual inferiors had the power to keep him from his birthright, or, if he minded his manners, to let him claim it. As a self-taught adult who was already in possession of the essentials of his *Weltanschauung*, there could have been little that so harassed him as the insistence of his patrons that he fill in the gaps of his formal schooling, the chief gap being his ignorance of Latin; for no *gymnasium* would give him a certificate of readiness to enter a university unless he had fulfilled that requirement. To his dismay and vexation, Hebbel found that he could not learn the rudiments of this language. His mind, soaring in the clouds of metaphysical speculation, could not stoop to master the declension of *ille, illa, illud.*

He did, of course, have friends and associates with whom he discussed literary and philosophical matters, but as he grew in intellectual stature, they became less adequate. And one of them, a certain Leopold Alberti, worked to spoil his relationship to Amalie Schoppe, which was none too secure at its best. There is no doubt that Dr. Schoppe extended to Christian Friedrich the helping hand which lifted him up into a larger world; but at the same time she refused to let go and insisted upon leading and guiding him and directing the conduct of his life. Thus, when some weeks after his arrival in Hamburg he was faced with the necessity of finding a different place to live, it was she who obtained lodgings for him with a certain Mamsell Lensing, who lived with her mother and stepfather in a locality known as Am Stadtdeich. At the same time, Dr. Schoppe warned Hebbel that Mamsell Lensing's reputation was none of the best.

Why she did this is puzzling; for such a warning, she could surely have realized, might very well be self-defeating. Perhaps she thought that the effectiveness of the warning would be enhanced by the circumstance that Elise Lensing was more than eight years older than Hebbel and not very attractive. However that may be, no single event in Hebbel's life had a more fateful influence upon him than this action of Amalie Schoppe's.

As soon as Dr. Schoppe realized that her protégé's relations with Mamsell Lensing were not coldly formal, but that they both enjoyed cozy chats over afternoon coffee, she began to make frequent malicious allusions to their friendship. For the sake of appearances, Hebbel moved out of his quarters in Am Stadtdeich; but he did not cease to see Elise. The intimate afternoons were continued; indeed, they became essential to his life in Hamburg, for to Elise he could talk freely about all the things that were seething in his mind, and Elise could listen, agree, admire the brilliance of his reasoning, and accord with him in every way. Besides, Elise was a lady, had received training in good manners, could explain to him the mysteries of proper social behavior. In Hebbel Elise had met the great love of her life. For her no one else and nothing else mattered, and she asked nothing better than to love, obey, and comfort him. No sacrifice was too great, and it was for her a self-fulfillment when, later on, she could literally keep him alive with gifts or loans of money and clothing. It is indeed possible that without Elise Lensing, Friedrich Hebbel would never have attained the glory which he sought and won. In his diary, he writes: "Yesterday I moved out of Elise's house. I have every reason to set up a small monument to the six weeks which I spent with her, for, just as I was met by kindness immediately upon entering her home, I have taken love away with me. The girl is infinitely devoted to me. If my future wife loves me only half as much, I will be content."

After nearly a year of trying to confine his intellectual activity within the limits appropriate to a pupil at a *gymnasium*, Hebbel decided to move on to a university and applied for the rest of the sum which had been put at his disposal. The request was granted after much deliberation and despite the refusal of the rector of the Johanneum to give him a certificate of readiness. This meant that Hebbel could not be a regularly matriculated university student; but he accepted that consequence, and, after a visit to his mother in February, 1836, set off for Heidelberg, where he planned to be an auditor specializing in law.

Heidelberg turned out to be no great improvement over Hamburg. To be sure, he no longer had to endure being patronized, but neither did he receive free meals, and he had to be extremely prudent in the management of his pitiably meager resources. The Heidelberg students were somewhat foppish at this time, so that Hebbel had to wear the best shoes and clothing he had in order not to become the object of their malice. Even so, he was derided for wearing his hair long and unkempt, and would probably have run into serious trouble if he had not gained the status of a tolerated eccentric through turning out occasional verse for various acquaintances whom he would meet once a week in one of Heidelberg's many taverns.

These meetings were vital to him despite his extreme poverty, for, as he put it later, he needed to "consume people," that is, he had to have an audience listening to him as he explained or developed his ideas, for all through his life he was a compulsive conversationalist and always had a small circle of friends and admirers who hung, or at least pretended to hang, on his every word. These friends, however, did receive compensation, for the testimony is overwhelming and unanimous that Hebbel's conversations, or rather monologues, were brilliant, that he dealt with the most diverse and abstruse matters with virtuoso dexterity and sense of form. Among the friends in Heidelberg, in addition to three who had left Hamburg with him, two deserve special mention. One was Rudolf Ihering, who later made a name for himself in Romance Philology, and the other was Emil Rousseau, whose father held a responsible government post in Ansbach. These two young men, who had grown up in cultivated upper-middle-class circles, and who cherished the ambition of becoming known as writers, came to regard Klaus Friedrich Hebbel's son as their oracle. Ihering was rather quietly convinced by his father that he was not qualified to make his way as a poet, but between Hebbel and Rousseau there sprang up a profound friendship and love which was terminated only by the latter's untimely death.

In a letter to Elise (September 3, 1836), Hebbel tells how speedily Rousseau came under his spell: "When Rousseau met

me, he was a vehement follower of Schelling, an admirer of
Friedrich Rückert, a young man who sat in judgment upon
Goethe. After three days he called philosophy a blind nag,
Rückert a visionary, and Goethe the supreme God." In justice
to Hebbel it must be pointed out that he added: "This is all
very well, only too fast. Views of this sort do not grow out of
the ground like mushrooms, and I would be more content with
my treatment if it had given me more trouble."

Some of the time not spent in literary discussions with his
friends Hebbel devoted to writing various things with a view
to publication, and especially to mastering the craft of writing
novellas. Already in Wesselburen he had written various short
prose pieces, and in Hamburg he had written a novella entitled
"Barbier Zitterlein," a study of a man who, thwarted in his ambition to pursue a learned profession, becomes a barber and
finds consolation in a monomaniac love of his wife, and, upon
the wife's death, of his daughter. When the daughter marries
and has a child, the barber realizes his madness and begs to
be confined. In Heidelberg Hebbel composed a more tightly
organized and compact story called "Anna," about a maid-
servant who, ordered by her master to comb flax while the
other servants were amusing themselves at the fair, accidentally
upsets the candle which lights her work, thus setting fire to
the nobleman's mansion and the entire village. Anna, after
first allowing the fire to get out of hand, plunges into the flames.
Her remains are thrown into the carrion pit. Both stories show
Hebbel's predilection for the gruesome, but stylistically "Anna"
is superior to the earlier story in its detached presentation of a
sequence of terrible events. However, neither these nor any of
the other stories which Hebbel wrote, has any intrinsic merit.
In fact, prose narrative was never one of Hebbel's strong points.

The same cannot be said of certain lyric poems which he
composed in Heidelberg, notably the one called "Nachtlied," in
which is embodied one of Hebbel's basic experiences of life,
the individual's awe and dread of the Whole, which threatens his finite self. In supple melodious verses, the star-studded
night is shown to pulsate about the frightened man, who feels
that the monstrous force enveloping him is about to push him
into the abyss. But then sleep, the protector, approaches and
draws its encircling veil about him.

This poem was included in a collection which Hebbel wished to dedicate to his greatly admired Ludwig Uhland. He wrote Uhland about this, and when he received no answer to his letter, Hebbel was, of course, sorely disappointed. It later turned out that Uhland had never received Hebbel's request.

Hebbel had at least the two usual motives for wishing to see his writings published: for one thing, he coveted fame and, for the other, he was in great need of money. The funds which he had brought with him from Hamburg were being used up, largely for shoe repairs and lodging. It was by denying himself proper food that he effected his greatest economies, but at the cost of permanently undermining his health. Elise sent him sums of money from time to time and finally made a sizeable loan. The occasion was his decision to go to Munich.

From the beginning, Hebbel had been dissatisfied with his work in Heidelberg. The technical study of law bored and irritated him, and there was little stimulus from other sources. When, therefore, the one professor for whom he had any true respect counseled him to give up jurisprudence, he followed this advice very readily, even though he knew that his patrons in Hamburg would be indignant when they heard about it. Moreover, his friends from Bavaria, chiefly Rousseau, kept telling him that in Munich he could find the intellectual atmosphere he needed and that, besides, he could live there more cheaply. All these things prevailed upon him to accept Elise's money and go.

On September 12, 1836, he set out for Munich on foot, taking with him a jolly little dog which had been given him by Rousseau and which was to be his inseparable companion, even on a much longer and more difficult walking trip. He went first to Strassburg, to see the great cathedral and the countryside which had had such meaning for Goethe. From Strassburg he made his way to Stuttgart, where he called on Dr. Hermann Hauff, editor of the *Morgenblatt,* who encouraged him to send in articles from Munich. Being so near to Tübingen, he could not resist the desire to pay his respects to Uhland. This was, of course, a great moment for Hebbel, but, alas, it proved to be a bitter disappointment. Uhland in no respect resembled the ideal poet as Hebbel had envisaged him, but was shy, reserved, and somewhat inarticulate. Richer by one more sad experience, Hebbel pushed on to Munich, where he arrived on September 29, 1836.

II *Munich*

Hebbel spent three years in Munich, years that were rich in experiences of all kinds, years in which the germs of many of his plays came into being. He did not, however, actually begin writing plays until he was back in Hamburg. In Munich, his literary efforts, aside from some travel impressions which he submitted to the *Morgenblatt*, were devoted to lyric poetry and to attempts to master the novella-form, attempts which were largely unsuccessful.

He wrote such tales as "Schnock" (1836), a character sketch of a cowardly giant consisting of a long string of episodes illustrating Schnock's unbelievable poltroonery. Hebbel tried this technique again in "Der Schneidermeister Nepomuk Schlägel" (1837), the "hero" of which is presented to the reader as the personification of envy and self-dissatisfaction. The exact opposite of this technique was exhibited in the story "Herr Haidvogel und seine Familie" (conceived in 1836 or 1837, revised in 1847, and published in 1848). Here one change of fortune follows rapidly upon the other, so that the reader feels a certain interest in learning whether Herr Haidvogel, spendthrift and egotist, will be compensated for a squandered fortune by the inheritance of his wife's uncle's property.

A further development of this style may be seen in Hebbel's last novella, "Die Kuh" (1849), which is sometimes said to be his best contribution to the genre. It is a very short and dense story, the first half of which sets forth the conditions that lead to total disaster in the second. The farmer Andreas has finally managed to scrape together enough money to buy a cow. As he steps outside to see whether his wife is driving the animal home, he lights his pipe with a scrap of paper. In his brief absence, his little boy, imitating what he has just seen, lights one of the hard-earned bank notes after the other at the stove. Andreas returns, sees what has happened, and throws the boy against the wall, beating out his brains. Then he hangs himself. In the confusion following the discovery of the disaster, the house catches fire. Andreas' wife, swooning, dies in the fire by accident or design. And, finally, the terrified cow plunges into the burning building and also perishes. The story is remarkable for its speed, for the effectiveness of the exposition, and for the dramatic denouement in which one disaster follows the other, but, as it is scarcely necessary to point out, the effect is ludicrous rather than imposing. Hebbel wrote some other stories as well, notably the so-called Märchen "Der Rubin" (1837), which he later gave dramatic form.

In addition to writing novellas and tales, Hebbel continued to produce poems, most of them lyrics but some ballads and other short narratives. In November, 1837, he collected one hundred and thirteen poems which he asked permission to dedicate to Uhland. He did not receive Uhland's reply until February, 1838. The reply was friendly but held out no hope that Uhland's publisher, Cotta, would accept the work. Hebbel then turned to another publisher, Julius Campe, who likewise refused the collection, but showed the poems to Karl Gutzkow, who was the editor of Campe's journal, *Der Telegraph*. Gutzkow was favorably impressed and agreed to print some of them and thus to recommend Hebbel's other poems to the serious consideration of editors of other journals. Hebbel, however, who was always suspicious both of Gutzkow's judgment and his character, and who totally rejected the demand of the "Young Germany" group, which included Gutzkow, to enlist literature in the service of political ends, did not agree to the proposal.

In his reply to Hebbel, Uhland listed the ten poems he considered the best of the collection. In addition to "Nachtlied," which has already been considered, there were two or three others that might be mentioned, for example, "Bubensonntag," in which the poet tries to recapture, in a verse form that recalls the "Bergidylle" of Heine's *Harzreise*, the feelings he had when, as a small boy, he had to go to church early in the morning, both hoping and dreading that he would see God the Father. "Der junge Schiffer" is a hearty, strongly rhythmical expression of a young man's wish to voyage to distant places.

"Zwei Wanderer," in contrast to these two, is rather mysterious and obscure: a mute traveler is journeying through the world, bearing an unutterable message from God for someone he has never seen. A deaf traveler is journeying through the world, his ears sealed by God until the time he meets the man without speech. But when these two see each other, the mute will be able to speak and the deaf man will hear and decipher the message. Here Hebbel is apparently giving poetic form to an idea which he took from Schelling.[1] The mute stands for unconscious Nature, which has an unspoken message for Man, who is deaf. They will understand each other when, through the self-evolution of God, Mind, which has been imprisoned in Nature, attains freedom through becoming fully aware of itself. Despite Uhland's favorable comments, however, and in the light of Hebbel's later achievements in lyric and narrative verse, the poems from this period of his life, with the exception of "Die Nacht," do not impress us as being great.

One of the reasons for Hebbel's eagerness to have his poems published was his continuing poverty. For weeks at a time his diet would consist of nothing but bread and coffee. To Elise he wrote that the rolls he ate were at least tasty and that lack of food did not cause him as much worry as did his inadequate wardrobe. He had had his jacket turned, and his trousers looked completely worn out. It seemed at least possible that if his dress became still shabbier the police would deny him permission to continue living in Munich, and he felt envious of his dog, born with its clothing. Worst of all was the constant anxiety caused by his almost ragged appearance, and the loss of that peace of mind which is indispensable to intellectual productivity. He writhed at having to accept another loan from Elise. Instead of the cash which she wished to send, he asked her to have coat and trousers made for him, and he gave her his precise measurements and instructed her to dirty the garments a little so that he would not have to pay duty.

Some six weeks later he received a package containing jacket, trousers, vest, socks, and cravat, for Elise had disregarded his admonitions to be sparing and sent him a complete wardrobe for two years, as he said, protesting that never in his life had he owned such a fine suit. "Still," he wrote on December 7, 1837, "I must confess that I would have suppressed my wish [for a new coat] if I had suspected that you would fulfill it so magnificently. I know very well that you do not give gifts in order to have them reciprocated, that you do not wish to fetter but to liberate by means of your kindness, but I am so much the

more oppressed by my inability to show you how grateful I am.
I must, indeed, account it the greatest good fortune of my life
that our paths have crossed. In Hamburg, where no one understood me, you accorded me sympathy, incentive, and comfort,
you stood by my side in my worst hours and—you know that I
never felt at ease anywhere but in your house—you gave me
my most beautiful ones."

And so he went on in words which he knew would give Elise
cause to hope that he returned her love as she wished it returned.
But even as he assured her that no one had ever meant as
much to him as she did, he was careful to weave into the long
letter unmistakable indications that he did not wish their relationship to culminate in marriage. This was the reason for
writing in the preceding passage that Elise did not wish to fetter
but to liberate by means of her kindness. And a little farther
on in the same letter he writes: " . . . every feeling is sacred to
me, but I would like to arouse an immutable feeling in your
heart, and such a feeling is that of friendship." And he assures
her that she would only gain in his eyes if she could transform
her so-called stronger but forbidden feelings into the eternal
and immutable one, namely friendship.

For Elise, of course, the only immutable feeling was her love
for this man, a love she retained to the end of her life despite
Hebbel's fits of temper, his readiness to point out that she was
neither young nor beautiful, his vehement declaration that marriage would stifle him and put an end to his creative work.
Despite the arrogance and egotism which can be found in
many of his letters to Elise, there is no mistaking the tone of
desperate revolt against the claims of Elise's love upon his life
and person. Nor is there any mistaking his recognition of her
kindness, generosity, and single-minded devotion to him. At
the same time, of course, he was fully aware, and tormented by
the awareness, that, in view of his dread of marrying her he was
really exploiting and using her to gain his own ends. It is thus
not hard to see in the relationship of Hebbel to Elise Lensing the
prototype of a conflict which is found in a play like *Judith*, where
the Assyrian general Holofernes treats Judith as an instrument of
his lust, but loses his life to her.

Although during his years in Munich Hebbel wrote many
letters to Elise, little or no mention of her is made in the diary.

Instead, there are a good many references to his "dearest sweetest Beppi." This was Josepha Schwarz, the daughter of a carpenter named Anton Schwarz, who gave his name, unwittingly to be sure, to Meister Anton, the father in the play *Maria Magdalene*. Hebbel made the girl's acquaintance shortly after his arrival in Munich, and soon Beppi was showing him the places of interest in the city, taking him to services in the Catholic churches to hear the music, explaining the rituals of her church so far as she understood them. Before long she had no secrets from him at all, and had confessed that she had had another lover before Hebbel, an unworthy one. To this Hebbel apparently made the same reply he later put on the Secretary's lips in *Maria Magdalene:* "No man can get over that."

Very soon, when he realized her despair, Hebbel bitterly regretted his cruelty and unfairness, and in his diary he wrote: "How often do I pray from the depths of my soul: O God, why am I as I am? The most terrible thing!" Nonetheless he did not break off the affair and continued to take delight in his association with Beppi, but also to torment her with accusations of one kind or another, pretending to be in love with someone else or accusing her of having a merely sensual love for him. These accusations she staunchly denied, but at times when his cruelty became almost more than she could bear, she would resolve to leave him. "But then," she said on one occasion, "I remembered how many socks you had in need of mending, and I felt so sorry for you that I changed my mind."

Another name, almost the only other one, that frequently occurs in the diaries of the Munich years is that of his friend Emil Rousseau, whom he had left behind in Heidelberg. They exchanged letters faithfully and Rousseau told Hebbel how he had struggled to gain his father's consent to drop the study of jurisprudence for that of philosophy, with the idea of devoting his life to literature. Hebbel wrote to him of the hardships he would encounter on this road but was, of course, overjoyed when Rousseau came to Munich on April 13, 1837, for now he had someone to whom he could talk about the things which interested him most, literary problems, philosophical issues, the lectures at the university, particularly those of Schelling and Joseph Görres. Through Rousseau, who had family connections in Munich, Hebbel made some further acquaintances, notably a certain Franz Gartner. Gartner, a gifted amateur, frequently played the piano for him, and in this way he came to have some notion of music. Rather unexpectedly, he preferred Mozart to the other composers.

In August, 1838, Rousseau's studies culminated in the public defense of his thesis. He had, quite naturally, chosen Hebbel to be his opponent in the disputation, an office which gave Hebbel great satisfaction, partly because he could function thus officially on an occasion of social and intellectual significance, but especially because now he discovered that he could speak as readily before a large audience as before an audience of three or four. Rousseau subsequently returned to Ansbach to see his parents and rest a bit after his exertions. Hebbel was to follow him and spend some time in Ansbach also. But on September 16 he received news of his mother's death at the age of fifty-one, and some two weeks later, on October 4, he learned of the death of Rousseau, who had fallen ill on September 17 and died on October 2.

Hebbel was deeply shaken by his double loss. He could be somewhat philosophical about the death of his mother, who, as he said, never was able to understand him although she sensed his exceptional qualities. But Rousseau had been a part of his intellectual life, had contributed to his spiritual growth, and had loved him with the intensity of devotion which Hebbel both inspired in, and demanded of, those who were close to him. When he heard of the fatal outcome of Rousseau's illness, he was so shocked that it took him a long time to muster the courage to enter the mere fact in his diary; and it took him nearly a month to write a letter to Elise, telling her what had happened and how it had affected him. With the death of Rousseau, living in Munich lost its meaning for him. He was using up his little store of cash, had no prospects of earning anything by writing, and felt too depressed to spur himself into activity. Perhaps a change of scene, that is, a return to Hamburg, would help him, and he asked Elise's advice on this matter, adding that the decision must be made quickly, for winter was coming on, and he planned to walk through the heart of Germany from the south to the north.

The decision to return to Hamburg had been taken, but the weather made it necessary for him to delay his departure until spring. We do not know how this decision affected Beppi. She probably accepted it submissively and continued to love and comfort him as best she could, for he was now living in her parents' home. Toward the end of winter, Hebbel resolved to leave. "In very beautiful frosty weather," he writes in his diary, "at six in the morning on the eleventh of March, I left Munich. Beppi carried my knapsack to the end of Ludwigstrasse. There I took it on my back myself . . . Beppi walked with me for more than two hours. In a peasant tavern standing alone in the woods, the so-called cold shelter, we drank the last glass of beer together, then we parted with never-ending tears." Beppi trudged back to Munich, while he strode on to Hamburg followed by his little dog, the gift of Emil Rousseau.

CHAPTER 3

The Early Plays

I Judith

THE route which Hebbel had very carefully planned for his long walk took him through Ingolstadt, Eichstätt, and Schwabach to Nuremberg. He had his first experience of railroad travel on the short line from Nuremberg to Fürth, the first railway built in Germany. From Fürth he went on to Bamberg, Coburg, and Gotha, where he encountered cold and snow. Whenever he stopped at an inn to get a bite to eat for himself and his dog, the poor creature tried to keep its master from going on. Hebbel was sometimes forced to carry it because the frozen roads and snow had cut its paws.

When he arrived in Göttingen, Hebbel consulted the university directory and found the name of Rudolf Ihering, whom he had known slightly in Heidelberg and had encountered again briefly in Munich. It cannot be said that Ihering was happy to see him. He looked more like a journeyman laborer than a student, with his rough, heavy clothing, and shoes that were in need of repair. All the same, Hebbel was so obviously in need of help that Ihering put him up for a few days to rest and recuperate, had his shoes resoled, and gave him some money to continue his journey. Hebbel apparently needed to talk just as much as he needed to rest. "He lectured, lectured constantly," Ihering later recalled, "and when, after one such rather long lecture, I expressed my appreciation for the pleasure and stimulus which he had afforded me, he replied that he had been talking not so much on my account as in order to clarify his ideas. I had served him only as a sounding board! . . . Hebbel my guest, and urgently dependent upon my support, and I readily subordinating myself to him and acknowledging his superiority, and then such an unexpected slap in the face!"

After the pause in Göttingen, Hebbel went on to Hanover, Celle, and Soltau, where his little dog became so ill that he nearly despaired of its life. The last night of the trip he had to spend in a peasant's cabin on a dirty bed among unfriendly people. Before noon the next day he reached Harburg outside Hamburg, where he waited for Elise, who came by the afternoon steamer. On March 31, 1839, he was back in Hamburg.

At first, of course, there was a sense of strangeness between him and Elise, but after a while he had accustomed himself to his old surroundings, and things seemed to be going well. Dr. Schoppe had received him kindly, and he had made new acquaintances in her home. He had become personally acquainted with Gutzkow, who was friendly and expressed his readiness to accept literary contributions from him. He felt justified in complimenting himself upon the progress he had made in the years he had been away. He was now able to be at ease with the leading intellectual lights of Germany. The future seemed for a while to look less gloomy than it had, but then he fell dangerously ill of pneumonia. Elise nursed him through the illness, and he recovered rather quickly, but he was left weak, discouraged, and irritable. Friction began building up between him and Dr. Schoppe, who vigorously disapproved of his liaison with Elise. He was not, however, so downcast that he could not submit some critical articles to *Der Telegraph*, even though he continued to doubt Gutzkow's sincerity. And it was a great solace to him that Ludwig Tieck wrote an appreciative letter about the sketch "Schnock," which Hebbel had sent him. In this letter, he expressed the hope that Hebbel would soon be inspired to write a larger work. This hope came true soon afterwards: on October 2, 1839, Hebbel began work on his first drama, the tragedy *Judith.*

Autumn was always Hebbel's productive season, and over and over again he was to find that his poetic vein would start to flow at that time, more or less as if some faculty within him were functioning independently. But about three weeks after he had begun composition of the play he was seriously distracted: the smoldering friction between him and Dr. Schoppe burst into a flame which excited and enraged him.

The occasion of the trouble was Hebbel's disappointment with a position which Amalie Schoppe had found for him. She had

asked him whether he would like to take over the review editor-
ship of the Dresden *Abendzeitung,* the editor of which was
Theodor Hell, a pseudonym for Karl Gottlieb Theodor Winkler.
Hebbel said he would be interested. Theodor Hell was not
opposed to the idea, but pointed out that because he and Hebbel
had such opposite views they would have to come to an understanding about policy. Hebbel, who wanted complete autonomy,
immediately rejected the whole idea. Dr. Schoppe was offended.
Hebbel remained firm. Then he returned an old copy of Dr.
Schoppe's journal, *Pariser Modeblätter,* and received an indignant letter rebuking him for having badly soiled and torn the
magazine, and requesting the return of all the books she had
lent Hebbel to "preserve them from a similar fate." Hebbel,
furious, noted in his diary that the journal was not soiled and
torn; at the most it was dusty and might have had some
coffee stains. The quarrel continued for some time with attempts
at arbitration being made by interested friends, attempts which
failed when Dr. Schoppe accused Hebbel of having snubbed her
and her mother on the street. But then a reconciliation did take
place towards the end of November, so that Hebbel, looking
back over the year just past, felt somewhat easier about his
relations with the *Frau Doktor.* At no time, however, was he
able to look at the whole affair as the trivial and childish thing
it seems to us.

The year 1839 ended on a more hopeful note. Hebbel was
able to record in his diary December 31 that he had completed
two acts of *Judith* and that the other three were planned down
to the last detail. And then, reviewing in his mind the personages
who had affected his life during the past year, he wrote: "Elise
Lensing (I write her name out in full because I am aware that
I have never mentioned her in my diary as she deserves to be
mentioned) is my good genius, and that Doctor Schoppe, who
placed me in her house, could so cruelly slander her on the basis
of vile washerwomen's gossip, is the sin which I find it hardest
to forgive. It is Elise, who, by sacrificing all her scanty resources,
maintained me both in Heidelberg and Munich, and asked for
no other reward than a not too unfriendly letter. What I received through the help of Doctor Schoppe would not have
maintained me in poverty for a year; Elise sacrificed herself, em-
broidered and sewed day and night, and was happy if she could

relieve my most pressing needs. Pure, heavenly soul, . . . only for your sake, only to secure you against a situation which will necessarily smother you, do I wish for a future that will give me more than a piece of bread for my own stomach! I have often been so cruel to you, caused you to shed so many a tear: if God forgives me this, I will have no need to fear anything else. You are a saint in my eyes, but saintliness provokes revolt as often as it compels adoration." It was not only in this diary entry that Hebbel expressed his sense of guilt and sin against Elise: the passage clearly foreshadows one aspect of the problem of tragic guilt in Hebbel's second play, *Genoveva*.

Judith was completed in about four months on January 27, 1840, a remarkable achievement for an inexperienced playwright. He sent one copy of the privately printed play to Uhland and one to Tieck, asking for their opinions of the work but, to his bitter disappointment, he received no reply. It is doubtful whether the play would have attracted attention had not Amalie Schoppe, now in one of the intervals of friendly feeling towards Hebbel, sent a copy to Auguste Stich-Crelinger, a prominent Berlin actress. Mme. Crelinger was enthusiastic about the play and the role of Judith as a vehicle for herself. To be sure, the play would have to be cut and altered somewhat for performance. Although Hebbel defended his work, he agreed to make changes in deference to expert practical opinion. Surprising though this readiness may seem, Hebbel never lost it, even after he had become famous as a playwright: recognition was worth the compromise and, besides, his true intent as well as his artistic achievement would be on permanent record in the printed editions of his works.

Even in a rather mutilated form, *Judith* was a success and brought Hebbel to the attention of the literary world. Quite possibly its success was due to the fact that, despite the seriousness of purpose, it is a sensational problem play, a sex melodrama, based, of course, on the apocryphal Book of Judith.

Hebbel took some liberties with the bare facts of his source, the most remarkable and not especially convincing one concerning the social status of his heroine. In the biblical account, Judith is a wealthy widow, the capable and presumably mature manager of a great inheritance. Hebbel's Judith is a little more than seventeen years old, not really a widow and not really a virgin, but both at the same time. This unusual condition Hebbel believed to be necessary because a widow, having experienced the conjugal embrace, could not even think of encompassing the death of a man in the way Judith did. Only a virgin ignorant of the meaning of the deed could imagine herself resolute enough to perform it. On the other hand, a true virgin would not be able to sacrifice that which constitutes her being, namely her virginity. Therefore, so ran Hebbel's logic, it was necessary to represent Judith as a virgin widow. Not quite fourteen years old, she was married to Manasseh and was taken to his home. Feverish with excitement, she awaited the consummation of her marriage, but it never took place: Manasseh, warned by some mystic signs, was able neither to touch her nor to explain what had happened to him. He died unexpectedly after about six months of this unnatural wedlock and left Judith on the one hand wondering whether some maleficent force dwelt within her and, on the other hand, despising men as weaklings, while longing for the embraces of one who would have the force to subject her to his will and desires.

Such is the confession she makes to Mirza, her servant, who had apparently been in ignorance of the true facts all along. Suddenly Ephraim, who loves Judith and wishes to marry her, bursts in upon them with the news that Holofernes, Nebuchadnezzar's great general, has laid siege to their city of Bethulia. In order to frighten Judith into his arms, Ephraim paints a terrifying picture of Holofernes, which only serves to make her reveal her hidden desire to find the man who will compel her admiration. When Ephraim persists with his suit, she bids him go and kill Holofernes; then he may claim the reward he desires. The mere suggestion terrifies Ephraim. Judith heaps contemptuous reproaches upon him, saying that, since all men are cowards, a woman has the right to do great deeds. She fasts in sackcloth and ashes for three days and nights, awaiting divine inspiration in answer to her prayer. One inspiration drives all other thoughts from her mind, but this inspiration she feels she must reject because of its sinfulness. But then she suddenly asks herself whether it is not God's will that she save His chosen people by means of a sin, whether she has the right to cherish her virgin purity more than the love of God. With that her resolution is made to gain access to Holofernes by means of her beauty, and she prays to God not to let her see any trace of goodness in him.

Meanwhile the plight of the city becomes rapidly worse. The water supply has been cut off, and some of the citizens begin to feel that anything would be better than dying of thirst. One of them, Assad, has a blind and mute brother named Daniel whom he has cared for and nursed throughout his life. Assad calls upon the Elders to open the gates and appeal to Holofernes' mercy. The mute Daniel suddenly is able to speak and cries out to the bystanders to stone Assad, and he castigates the people in the name of the Lord for their lack of faith.

Another citizen, Samaja, tries to help Assad, but in vain. Judith comes by in time to hear Samaja denouncing Daniel, who is once again mute, as if possessed by an evil demon. Samaja would have the people believe that the Lord would not cause the dumb to speak in order for them to bring about the death of a brother, and proclaims that what is against nature is against God. Judith, however, seeing in the miracle a pledge that the sin she is about to commit will find favor with the Lord, calls out, "Will you dictate to the Lord the path He must take? Does He not make clean every path which He takes?" In the tumultuous debate which ensues, Judith demands of the people that they obey the will of God. It is apparent, however, that she herself has impure motives, that she is drawn to Holofernes as woman is drawn to man, even though she has never seen him. When Achior, who had once been a captain of the Moabites, subject to Holofernes, declares that nothing will be gained by throwing open the gates and appealing to Holofernes' mercy, since he has vowed that he will exterminate the Jews, Judith questions Achior about Holofernes and inflames herself by means of Achior's account both of Holofernes' grandeur and of his contempt for women. Impelled by resentment against the tyrant male as much as by submission to the will of God, Judith prevails upon the Elders to let her leave the city.

She succeeds in reaching Holofernes' tent unmolested, for her beauty evokes a sense of awe even in the hardened soldiers of the Assyrian army. Holofernes grants her an audience. She tries, in various ways, to persuade Holofernes to spare her people, but he resists her wiles. Finally, she tells him that her god has resolved to punish the Hebrews through her agency, and that she will deliver them into Holofernes' hands within five days. This is agreeable to Holofernes, who gives her the freedom of the camp so that she may come and go unmolested.

As the stipulated five-day interval draws to its close, we see Holofernes in his tent soliloquizing about the pleasures of bending a woman to his will. He sends for Judith and engages her in a conversation concerning her feelings towards him. Torn between a kind of horrified love for Holofernes and rage at his indifference to everything about her save sexual attractiveness, she confesses that she hates him, but to no effect. At this point, Ephraim secures admittance to the tent under the pretext of important business. Having first secured Holofernes' promise not to take his life, he makes a foolish attempt to assassinate him. Holofernes spares his life, but orders him to be put into a monkey cage and taught the tricks of the former occupant. Judith thinks this magnanimous and prays to the god of her fathers to protect her so that she will not be compelled to honor what she loathes.

Holofernes then talks at length of his worship of power and confesses that it is terrible to be surrounded by such weaklings that he can honor no one except himself. Judith admits that she is stunned by what she has heard and unable to understand it. When Holofernes replies that she has the right to laugh at him, because it is foolish to try to explain such things to a woman, Judith, enraged, cries out, "Learn to have respect for women. A woman stands here to kill you! And she tells you this." This does not impress Holofernes, who says that she has made the admission in order to make the deed impossible. "In order to protect myself against you, I need only to get you with child." After drinking another cup of wine, Holofernes decides that the right moment has come and takes Judith by force into the inner tent, leaving Mirza behind in terrible suspense and fear. Presently, Judith returns in a dreadful state and tells Mirza of her outraged feelings, how her "senses, like drunken slaves, who no longer recognize their master, revolted against her," and she "began to take all her past life for a mere proud dream, and her disgrace for her true life." Upon this follows the brutal rape, and it is the thought of this that gives her strength to return to where Holofernes lies sleeping and chop off his head.

When she and Mirza return to Bethulia with Holofernes' head in a sack, when it becomes known what she has done, and when blind panic breaks out in the camp, which allows the Hebrews to slaughter the Assyrians, there is great rejoicing in the city. The Elders ask Judith to name her reward. She, to their amazement, exacts from them the promise to kill her if she demands this of them. To Mirza she explains: "I do not wish to bear Holofernes a son! Pray to God that my womb will be barren. Perhaps He will be merciful." But whether merciful or not, Judith has killed the one man she might have loved, the only one who could have given meaning to her life. She was the instrument of God's will, but, by virtue of being human, she was an imperfect instrument. This imperfection, the common lot of all individuals, wrought her doom. Such, in Hebbel's view, is the nature of tragedy, which is inevitable in human life.

Judith's tragedy is thus not simply her personal experience, the unique case, which, interesting though it may be, sheds little light on the human predicament, but, so Hebbel would have us believe, it helps to make understandable how the very life process is inevitably tragic for each individual. More than this, since Judith and Holofernes are representatives of their people, the play, in Hebbel's view, gives us an insight into the metaphysics of history. In a diary entry dated April 3, 1840, which is a revision of a letter to Mme. Stich-Crelinger of the same date, Hebbel writes: "Judith and Holofernes are, if I was successful, not only individuals, but also the representatives of their people. Judith is the dizzy peak of that people which believed it stood in a personal relationship to the very Deity, and Holofernes is paganism over-reaching itself and on the brink of a precipice. In all his might, he grasps the ultimate idea of history, the idea of a god to be born from the womb of humanity, but he attributes a demiurgic power to his thoughts and believes that he is what he thinks he is. Judaism and paganism, on the other hand, are only representatives of humanity, which, from the very beginning, is split in an irreparable dualism. Thus the struggle in which the elements of my tragedy grind each other to pieces has the highest symbolic significance, although it is kindled by passion and is terminated by tumult of the blood and the misguiding power of the senses."

Here Hebbel touches upon one of the most significant and persistent of his ideas, the concept of a dualism which makes it possible for the individual to become differentiated from the

Absolute, the Idea, or, in religious terminology, God. The undifferentiated Idea, the Whole, if it could exist, would necessarily be lifeless and rigid. "Life," he wrote in his diary on February 2, 1841, "is the effort of the rebelliously defiant part to tear itself loose from the Whole and to exist by itself, an effort that is successful for the duration of the energy of which the Whole has been robbed by means of the separation of the individual." When this energy has been consumed, the individual must inevitably lose his individuality through being reabsorbed into the Whole, a necessarily tragic process which constitutes the central problem of both philosophy and art, especially drama. Philosophy, however, must fail in its task to determine the cause of this process, for that cause is unfathomable. No one who seeks earnestly to learn the cause can find it. But the drama accepts individuation as a prime factor in life and seeks only to show how the metaphysical breach is healed, namely through the tragic process.

When Hebbel wrote to Mme. Stich-Crelinger that Judith stood for Judaism and Holofernes for paganism, he really pointed to the weakness of his work as a creative writer, namely a hyperintellectualism which sometimes caused him to write in a conceptual rather than a presentational mode. Because of the intellectual's unfortunate tendency to attribute greater reality to the abstract than the concrete, a character such as Holofernes never comes to life, but serves only as a vehicle for Hebbel's ideas. Because Holofernes is supposed to represent the excessive cruelty of a polytheism so extreme that it deifies the individual (for example, Nebuchadnezzar's proclamation of his own divinity), and conceives the idea of a god to be born of mankind, he becomes merely ludicrous.

A good example of this comes in the fourth act, where Holofernes is complaining to Judith of the excruciating boredom of his lot: there is no one who would dare oppose him, for Nebuchadnezzar has only the semblance of power. But if he should decide to feed Nebuchadnezzar to the tigers of Assyria, then humanity would recognize in him, Holofernes, its god. "Oh, the last moment, the last, if only it were already here! 'Come here, everyone whom I have hurt,' I will cry out, 'you whom I crippled, you whose wives I have torn from your arms and whose daughters I have torn from your side, come and devise torments for me! Tap my blood and give it to me to drink, cut flesh from my loins and give it to me to eat!' And when they believe they have done the worst possible things to me and I suggest something still worse and ask them pleasantly not to keep that from me, when they stand around me in horrified amazement and I, in spite of all my pain, smile them into death and madness: then I will thunder to them, 'Kneel down, for I am your god,' and I will close my lips and eyes and die in peace and secret." Such a rodomontade, designed to make us believe in Holofernes as the symbol of paganism overreaching itself and going down in self-destruction, can only invite parody.

Despite its weaknesses, the play was acted with considerable success with Mme. Stich-Crelinger as Judith, on July 6, 1840. Hebbel was now fairly started on the road to fame and moderate fortune, but many struggles and hardships still lay before him on this road, not the least agitating of which was the final break with Amalie Schoppe.

Although Dr. Schoppe had, as we know, interested Mme. Stich-Crelinger in *Judith*, the hostility between her and Hebbel continued to mount until on May 4, 1840, she wrote him a letter which, in Hebbel's words (diary entry for May 20), "could have killed him," and he wondered whether he ought not to take legal action against her for her "attempted moral assassination." But finally he drew up a *pro memoria*, in which he traced the history of his relations with her and once and for all declared his independence. It is not known precisely what Dr. Schoppe had written in her letter which so agitated Hebbel, but it seems that she must have accused him of ingratitude for the benefactions he had received through her, saying that she had gotten along very well without him, and that he would now have to get along without her. In a terrible fury, he counted up all the benefactions he had received through her agency and demonstrated that he had in fact been independent of her and his other patrons since 1836. To whom, then, did he owe the indispensable means of subsistence? "You have tried so hard to find out what my relationship has been to Fräulein Lensing. I will tell you now: it was the relationship of a human being to his protecting spirit! This woman, whose nobility of soul and kindness of heart are without parallel, at least in my life, and acquaintance with whom I do indeed owe to you, of her own free will extended a saving hand when I was reduced to extremities in Heidelberg. Little by little, she advanced me a total of 500 Reichstaler. Indeed, in order to relieve my mind of its most oppressive worry, with my knowledge, she sent my mother the rent which was due semi-annually. And more than that, without my knowledge, she made her happy with presents of money and other things which she sent her in my name, as if she were only an intermediary."

Although Hebbel's relationship to Elise might very well be characterized as that of a human being to his guardian angel, it was, in fact, much more complex than that and considerably more guilt-ridden, for Elise was with child. This was, of course, a disturbing situation in any case, since her income was small and Hebbel's almost non-existent. Worse than that, Hebbel felt himself bound with a bond more powerful than gratitude to a woman to whom, despite or even because of her devotion, he did not wish to be bound, as he surely did not wish to be bound to the drab social and literary circles which had up to this time been open to him. But now, as the author of a play that had caused a considerable stir, he was gaining *entré* to more glittering social circles, in which, for example, a professor from Russia appeared, or the very delightful daughter of a certain Senator Schröder of Hamburg.

To Elise, who was absent from Hamburg for what may be presumed to have been urgent personal reasons, Hebbel wrote on July 19, or 20: "On Saturday I had a very enjoyable day at Mme. Hellberg's. Lawyer Schütze was there . . . Also Miss Emma Schröder, who made an impression on me such as few girls have made. Since the day when I first saw this lovely creature, I have been in a state of intoxication, my heart bubbling over, and my head too. You will be happy about this, when I tell you that I was close to inner suffocation. . . . Now I am free again and am producing something. A person such as I am has his own conditions of existence; he cannot lead a conventional life. He must reach out high and low and, to be sure, he often devours people. We drank to your health. I took Miss Schröder home. Do you mind? I am sure you don't."

Hebbel could not possibly have been so simple-minded as to suppose that the woman who was about to bear his child would look with sympathetic interest upon his love affair with someone else. It seems more likely that he was brutally impressing upon Elise that she should not cherish any hope of marrying him. Hence his praise of love, a feeling so different from the friendship which he professed for Elise, and which he recommended to her as the proper form for their relationship to take, so different from his relationship to Beppi Schwarz, which he now said he must break off.[1] As if to leave no doubt of his meaning, he wrote, "It is really true, love is something different from friendship, and it is also true that love is drawn to youth and beauty." If he did not go on to point out that Elise was not strikingly endowed with either youth or beauty, it was only because he remembered that he had already done so.

At other times (September 3, 1840) Hebbel could write: "I would like to kneel before you the whole day long and beg your forgiveness for having tormented you so often, wounded you to the depths, bitterly reviled you. Oh, there is often such confusion in my nature that my better self, timid and frightened, strays about among these chaotic and conflicting streams of violence and passion. My lips are then in the pay of demonic forces which have subdued me and, pressed back into my innermost self sits my soul, like a child that cannot speak for weeping and shuddering. . . ." Out of his struggle to understand and justify himself in his deliberate compulsion to injure and defile grew the character of Golo in his next play, *Genoveva*.

In the course of time, Hebbel's ardor for Emma Schröder was diminished, and she disappeared from his life. On November 5, his first son was born. It was a difficult birth, and Elise's recovery was doubtful. To add to the cares and anxieties of this period, Hebbel was forced to borrow money from Emil Rousseau's father to repay Kirchspielschreiber Voss for his mother's funeral expenses. And *Judith* was performed in Hamburg.

Through all the emotional turmoil, Hebbel's poetic vein had been running: on March 1, 1841, after five and one-half months of work, *Genoveva* was completed.

II Genoveva

The legend of Saint Genevieve has been traced back to the fourteenth century, but it was not until the seventeenth that it attained the popularity of a chap-book in the version of the French Jesuit René de Cerisiers, entitled *L'Innocence reconnue*, *ou Vie de Sainte Geneviève de Brabant.* Young Hebbel seems to have known a German version of this chap-book. At any rate, the story figures in his earliest dramatic plans. His interest in it was renewed in Munich through reading the play *Golo und Genoveva* by the Storm-and-Stress writer Friedrich (better known as Maler) Müller, which stimulated him to making a sketch of the action and characters as he would wish to have them. But the immediate impetus to composing his play seems to have come to Hebbel from reading the play *Leben und Tod der heiligen Genoveva* by Ludwig Tieck, which he criticized as severely as he did Müller's version

The outline of Hebbel's plot is quite simple. Siegfried, Count Palatine, setting out for the wars against the Moors in the early eighth century, leaves his possessions and his beloved wife, Genoveva, in the charge of his favorite, Golo. Golo, to whom Genoveva had seemed a saint devoid of human feelings, witnesses the leave-taking. To his amazement, he sees that Genoveva is capable of sensual ardor. A wild passion is kindled in him. For a while after Siegfried's departure Golo half tries to suppress his desire, but before long he confesses his love for Genoveva and pleads with her to requite it. She refuses, and Golo's love gradually turns into cruel and ruthless determination to force Genoveva to accept him as a lover. When she persists in her refusal, he contrives to make her seem guilty of adultery with Drago, a simple retainer, and has her locked up in a dungeon on bread and water. Here she bears Siegfried's child.

News comes of Siegfried's imminent return. Golo goes to meet him in Strassburg, where he is resting to recuperate from badly healing wounds. Golo convinces Siegfried that Genoveva has been unfaithful. Siegfried authorizes Golo to effect her execution. After trying once more to seduce Genoveva, Golo orders the retainers Hans and Balthasar to kill her in the forest. The imbecile Klaus goes with them. Hans tries to make Klaus kill Genoveva, but instead Klaus kills Hans. Balthasar becomes convinced of the possibility of Genoveva's innocence and allows her to escape with her son. He then pretends to Golo that Genoveva is dead. Golo, in a fury, kills Balthasar. Then Caspar, the best of the retainers, arrives with Siegfried. Golo and Caspar, who also knows of Genoveva's innocence, allow Siegfried to persist in his belief in Genoveva's guilt. Siegfried allows Golo to leave his service and departs. Golo now punishes himself by putting out his eyes and asks Caspar to leave him to the wild beasts. Caspar, however, mercifully dispatches him with his sword. This was the end of the play until January, 1851, when Hebbel added an epilogue in which Siegfried, out hunting, pursues a hind to a cave where Genoveva and her son have been living for seven years on the milk of the hind and such fruits of the wilderness as they could gather. Genoveva's saintliness is thus demonstrated, and she is restored to her huband. It is plain, however, that she has only a very short time to live.

Hebbel was never really satisfied with *Genoveva*. No sooner had he completed it than he realized the need of making considerable alterations. His own analysis of its weakness was entered in his diary on May 29, 1841: "The flaw of the play is the flaw of its idea, and that, to be sure, is the worst flaw it can have. This idea is the Christian one of expiation and atonement by saints." The consequence of the idea is that Genoveva is a completely passive character   The play cannot, therefore, be the tragedy of Genoveva but must be her glorification. Genoveva is, at the beginning of the play, a fully developed character, who remains untouched by the trials and temptations to which she is subjected. Indeed, she is all but identified with God, so that Golo can call upon her to speak for Him. To be sure, she suffers in both body and spirit from Golo's mad love and equally mad cruelty, but her goodness is so perfect that there is never any doubt about the outcome and, therefore, no feeling of suspense. At most there is a feeling of indignation or wonderment or sadness that a flawless woman must be subjected to such persecution.

It is, therefore, Golo who is the protagonist of the play and the main point of interest, even though he is scarcely a more dramatic hero than is Genoveva, for he has no human opponent except himself. He does develop, it is true, but by a process which might be characterized as the self-explication of a polysyllogism or sorites. By logical consequence, his potentialities for evil are unfolded, with himself supplying the motive force, or rather, the compulsive force, for he sees clearly what is happening to him and is horrified by himself, but is unable and unwilling to stop or alter the course of events. "A man al-

ready is what he can become," he says in a passage which
Hebbel omitted from the play.

The realization that Genoveva is capable of human love gives
him his first inkling of his capacity for sin. Genoveva faints
when Siegfried tears himself away, leaving her supported in
Golo's arms. Golo kisses her while she is still unconscious. When
she recovers, he hints that Siegfried is not worthy of her love,
immediately realizes where this act, insignificant in itself, will
lead him, and prepares to climb a tower which no one has ever
successfully climbed. He motivates this seemingly insane act
by saying that he wishes to destroy a nest of jackdaws that
disturb Genoveva by their noise. In fact, he is literally tempt-
ing Providence by making a metaphysical experiment to determine God's will, and he prays God not to protect him. If he
returns safe to the ground, it will be a sign that he is meant
to be a scoundrel. He does return unharmed and is sure that
God performed a miracle in order that his villainy may become
complete. He is shaken to the depths when Genoveva suggests
that God may have performed the miracle because He will
have need of Golo later, but neither this nor any other consideration halts or impedes the growing fury of his passion. This
knowledge is imparted to the reader or spectator in a number
of inordinately long asides which convey the further insight that
Golo is near to killing Genoveva in self-defense. That is, Golo
feels that by merely being in her presence he is forced to become a criminal, and he prays to God to take her up into heaven:
she is like a great treasure of gold and jewels which makes a
thief of everyone who sees it.

So far Golo has been so much the inexperienced boy that he
has been unable to declare his love; but then a painter comes
with a portrait he has made of Genoveva. In her presence,
Golo loses himself in the contemplation of the picture and
finally reveals his love by kissing it. When he asks Genoveva
whether a man who knows that he is certain to become a great
criminal has the right to take his own life to prevent this, she
replies that nobility of soul must make it impossible for him
to do that which he condemns. But Golo swears that he is
capable both of committing the greatest of sins against her
and of taking his own life, if she, speaking for God, will sanction
his suicide. This she cannot do, and Golo, throwing away his

sword, breaks into wild protestations of love and denunciations
of Siegfried for his failure to know her worth. Genoveva ap-
peals to Golo's better nature by refusing to summon help, but
he, now that he has become a scoundrel, claims the rights of
a scoundrel, and is about to do her violence, when he is interrupted by the entrance of Katharina, an old woman who was
once his nurse. Now, aided and abetted by Katharina's sister,
a witch, he makes Genoveva seem guilty of adultery with
Drago. If she is thus dishonored, so the plotters reason, she
will be forced to purchase the semblance of honor by yielding
to Golo. When this plot fails, the next remaining steps are for
Golo to imprison Genoveva, and when Siegfried's return becomes imminent, to arrange for her execution, and, finally, as
we have seen, to inflict the most terrible punishment upon himself.

There is thus no dramatic conflict or struggle in the play, at
least in a sense, for Golo and Genoveva are not really oppo-
nents. Each is actually only the occasion for revealing the
other's true nature, even though each is necessary for the fulfillment of the other's destiny. They are thus both seen to be
in the grip of the highest power, that is, God, and Genoveva
is actually God's representative. As we have seen, Golo understands that. Therefore, when Golo persists in his passion for,
and persecution of, Genoveva, he is really challenging God; and,
in the metaphysical sense, the dramatic and tragic conflict in
the play is between Golo and God, a conflict which can end in
only one way: the destruction of the individual. The role of
Genoveva in the metaphysical conflict is, therefore, seen to be
that of the instrument which God allows Golo to use in order
to destroy himself. On the other hand, an instrument so used
cannot but be broken. This means that for Genoveva, too,
even though she is God's representative, God is the ultimate
Adversary.

Thus it can be seen that the basic structure of the play has
been made to bear a great deal of metaphysical weight, in fact,
much more than has thus become apparent from this discussion, which has taken no account of a considerable number of
less prominent characters and a good many minor episodes.
These characters and episodes provide what might be called
the historical background, save for the fact that for Hebbel his-

tory is not the background of the drama but its native element. Two quotations will amplify this statement. "Just as every crystallization depends upon certain physical conditions, so does every individualization of human stuff [*des menschlichen Wesens*] depend upon the historical epoch in which it occurs. To exhibit these modifications of human nature in their relative necessity is the main task which literature, as an art, has in relation to history; and here, if it is successful in giving a true representation thereof, it can produce a supreme achievement" (diary entry for December 24, 1846). "Moreover, every drama is vital only to the extent that it serves to give expression to the time in which it is produced, that is, to the loftiest and truest interests of the time. . . ." (Preface to *Genoveva*). Thus *Genoveva*, being set in a semi-mythical medieval Christian age, must be faithful to the spirit of that age and must also reflect Hebbel's own age in the mirror of the medieval setting, which included not only the struggle between Christians and Moslems, but also witchcraft, the savagery of religious intolerance, a feudal social structure, Catholic forms of worship, and such figures as the imbecile Klaus, the knight Tristan, who was liberated from slavery through the love of a Saracen maid, and the Jew who is stoned for drinking from a public fountain from which a mangy dog has just drunk. These are all crystallizations of the human stuff which depend upon the historical conditions.

Historical conditions at this time were extremely critical for Christendom, for the great confrontation between Moslem might under Abd-er-Rhaman and Christian might under Charles Martel took place in the year 732 at the battle of Poitiers, in which the advance of the Moslems was stopped. Hebbel does not make use of this historical situation, although he was aware of it, but instead invents a myth which explains how Genoveva's full realization of saintliness serves a great cosmic purpose. According to this myth, which is told by the ghost of the murdered Drago, God promised in the beginning to spare the sinful human race if every thousand years only one individual should prove to be worthy. The end of the millennium is at hand, and mankind is wallowing in cruelty and sin so that annihilation is imminent. Upon Genoveva, therefore, depends the life or death of mankind: if she maintains her saintly purity,

God's purpose to redeem mankind through her will be realized. It need scarcely be pointed out that this makes of Genoveva a second Redeemer or Christ, and of Golo, an emissary or even the embodiment of Evil, for metaphysical Evil is identical with the sin of individuation. Golo's existence threatens God. He must, therefore, be allowed to destroy himself and save the world by helping Genoveva to realize her destiny.

One final complication in this overly complex drama requires our attention briefly. The modern historical problem which is mirrored in *Genoveva* is Hebbel's own personal problem, the relationship of man to woman, the sin of masculine egotism which reduces woman to the status of a thing, and also the demand of woman to become emancipated. We have seen it before in *Judith*, and we will encounter it again in Hebbel's other plays, for he never really solved it in his life.

CHAPTER 4

Royal Patronage

THE year 1841 was one of the most productive in Hebbel's life. He completed *Genoveva*, as we know, in March, and published *Judith* in July. Then he resumed work on a comedy, *Der Diamant*, which he had begun in Munich in February, 1838, and completed it by the end of November. After furnishing it with a prologue, he sent it to the management of the Hoftheater in Berlin to compete for a prize offered for the best modern comedy. It failed to win and Hebbel suspected that the panel of judges had probably not read it. This is quite possible, since the prologue is so polemical that the judges may very well have felt offended and thrown it out with no further ado. When the Poet in the Prologue—that is, Hebbel—tells the False Muse of his desire to write a comedy which will reveal the Spirit that rules the universe, the False Muse points out that that is not the way to win a prize, for the contemporaries want nothing from a comedy except topical and timely allusions, satirical barbs directed against the Church, the State, Society and well-known personalities. This kind of comedy, of course, is precisely what the Poet cannot and will not try to write. His intention is to show the illusion and futility of life by means of a diamond, which all who know about it struggle to possess, in their struggle revealing their true character. In Hebbel's view, comedy is fully as serious as tragedy.

In fact, tragedy and comedy are only two different forms of the same idea, he wrote in his diary on November 29, 1841. And the tragic side of comedy is, "for anyone who discovers it in the midst of the motley masks and arabesques which veil it, almost more terrible than tragedy itself" (from a letter to Charlotte Rousseau of July 7, 1843). And comedy, no less than tragedy, reflects the original cosmic dualism, for it depicts mankind in its "inevitable aberrations and abnormities, in its base inclinations and endeavors" (review of Ludolph Wienbarg, *Die Dramatiker der Jetztzeit*, September, 1839, Wke. X, 367).

The diamond, to which the title of Hebbel's comedy refers, has been in the possession of a royal family ever since the days of Frederick Barbarossa, when a phantom crippled soldier gave it to the ancestor of the present King. Superstition has it that the ring, which has been entrusted by the King to his daughter for safe-keeping, is bound up with the welfare of the dynasty and the country: if the ring is lost, disaster threatens. Now it happens that the Princess, given to mystical dreaming, was frightened by the appearance of a mortally ill and crippled soldier. Believing him to be the ghost come back to claim his ring, she throws it to him and falls into a serious illness. The Prince, her suitor, sets out with his companion, the Count, to try to find the diamond; and the King offers immunity from questioning and the reward of a fortune for the return of the stone. The loss of the diamond thus is actually endangering the life of the Princess, the welfare of the dynasty, and the peace of the country; for the neighbor state is making preparations for war now that good fortune has apparently forsaken the royal family.

Meanwhile the flesh-and-blood soldier to whom the Princess threw the ring has died in the home of Jacob, a dull-witted and earthy but kindly and decent peasant. Jacob's wife, to whom the soldier has willed the ring, considering it of no value, threw it away, and only on second thought looked for it and kept it because it might some day amuse her still unborn child. Jacob suspects its worth and calls in a passing Jewish peddler, Benjamin, to appraise the stone. Benjamin, during Jacob's momentary absence from the room, swallows the diamond and runs away. Jacob pursues him. Benjamin encounters a debt-ridden doctor named Pfeffer and his chief creditor, Block. He asks the doctor for relief from the indigestion caused him by the diamond, which seems irretrievably lodged in his stomach. When Jacob arrives, the three haul Benjamin off before Judge Kilian and charge him with the theft of the diamond. Kilian has read the King's notice of a reward for return of the diamond; so now he, as well as his servant Jörg and the jailer Schlüter, join the group, who are doing their best to recover the stone by opening Benjamin's stomach. Various attempts are made until Schlüter lets Benjamin escape in order to be alone with him in the forest, where he can perform the operation himself. Fear, induced by the imminence of the surgical incision, has a greater emetic effect than all the medicines Benjamin has swallowed, and the diamond emerges into the light of day. The upshot is that after considerable pulling and tugging the diamond is restored to the royal family, and the reward goes to the person who deserves it, namely Jacob.

This play has never been deemed a success by anyone except Hebbel, and even he felt at times that it needed revision. At other times, however, as in a letter to Gustav Kühne, editor of the journal *Europa* (January 28, 1847) he defended it valiantly, writing, "According to my feelings, it is the best and surely the most original of my productions, a comedy, which, as free and independent as a tragedy, confronts the universe and seeks to overcome its dualism without the help of tragedy." We who are not so much in love with the ideas and the irony of the play as was Hebbel are likely to dismiss the whole thing as a case of indigestion in five acts. But the play does have more theoretical interest than that, and one can begin to understand why Hebbel, who delighted in the paradoxical and the grotesque, was captivated by his own creation.

The diamond, of course, has no intrinsic value, but means something different for each of the characters struggling to obtain it: to some it symbolizes the continuing welfare of the royal house and the state, to others, the means of saving a life threatened by fear of the supernatural, to still others, the means of satisfying greed, or release from poverty, and to Jacob, the possibility of doing good. Its effect on Benjamin is almost magic: it changes him from a human being into a piece of property, but at the same time he holds the fate of nations in his stomach. Despite its coarseness this last idea is really quite funny, but it must be detached from the play, that is, from the language of the play, in order to be effective. In brief, the play lacks wit, and all the characters sound as though they were expounding Hebbel's philosophy from a lecture platform.[1]

After completing *Der Diamant,* Hebbel turned to the task of getting a collection of poems ready for publication by Hoffmann and Campe. The two hundred and forty-eight page volume appeared in July, 1842, and contained several excellent poems. What has just been said about Hebbel's language in some of his plays cannot truly be said of his lyrics, or at any rate, of the best of them, even though they do mirror his view of life. In his really good poems, he achieves a persuasive sensuousness and succeeds in compressing his thought and feeling into symbolic images of great force. Such a poem from the collection of 1842 is "Sturmabend." In it, the poet addresses the wind on a stormy evening as it sweeps by him and his beloved. It loosens the rose from the girl's hair and blows it to the ground, where she tramples it underfoot as she embraces her lover; and she too feels a fiercer passion because of the storm. Both he and she feel that time is rushing away from them, as is the wind, but they have the courage of their ardor. Before him he sees the glowing crimson of her lips, two paces behind him is Death with lifted scythe. Here is expressed the essence of Hebbel's metaphysical dualism, the wild struggle of the individual to maintain itself in defiance of the Universal.

The collection of poems was not Hebbel's only publication of the year 1842: *Genoveva* appeared in print in October. The honorarium which he received for it he turned over to Elise; but then, in the fall, his poetic vein refused to flow. He had apparently reached the end of one stage and needed to take a decisive step in order to maintain his progress. The step which he had in mind was to go to Copenhagen and apply to His Majesty, Christian VIII, for financial support of some kind. This was not a hare-brained scheme, unlikely to succeed, for the kings of Denmark were known for their support of the arts, and Hebbel was, after all, a Danish subject. Besides, he had a powerful supporter in the person of Count Moltke, with whom he had become acquainted, and the Count had connections at the Danish court. So when Emil Rousseau's father made him a loan, and Campe, the publisher, advanced him twenty Louis d'ors, the venture looked promising enough to try. The trip to Copenhagen was a challenge and represented a brilliant opportunity to acquire social graces as well as the means to visit centers of culture and receive new impetus. Hebbel left Hamburg on November 12, 1842 by post-chaise for Kiel, where he boarded a ship for Copenhagen, arriving there on the fourteenth.

Here he lodged for a while in a good hotel, but very soon took a room in the apartment of a poor widow and her son in order to save money. In due course he presented himself to various dignitaries of the Danish court, through whose intercession he obtained his first audience with the King on December 13, 1842. According to his account to Elise, the audience lasted a fairly long time, perhaps because he had managed earlier to catch the King's interest by requesting the Marshal of the King's Household not to make an appointment for him until the King would have had time to read his writings. Marshal Levetzau had very courteously agreed to lay these writings before the King. When, therefore, after a sufficient interval had passed to allow King Christian to become familiar with Hebbel's works, Hebbel appeared before him, the basis for a conversation had been laid. At this time Hebbel asked the King for an appointment to the University of Kiel, where the professorship of esthetics was vacant. The appointment would have to be excepted, he explained, because he was not academically qualified. The King, however, was not in favor of this procedure, preferring to have him apply to the proper chancery officials, and switched the conversation to the subject of *Judith*, about which he had misgivings because of its indecent features. After Hebbel had assured the King that the objectionable matters were omitted from the acting version of the play, he bowed and took his leave, anticipating the wave of the hand which would have signified the termination of the audience. To Elise he wrote (January 14, 1843), defending his unconventional behavior, that, as far as ceremony was concerned, his model was Goethe in his audience with Napoleon.

At no other time in his life did he miss and need Elise as much as during his stay in Copenhagen, for to him she was the fount of knowledge of all things having to do with etiquette. The letters of introduction from Count Moltke had thrown open the doors of high society to the brick-layer's son, and he found himself dining in the company of the rich and well-born, whose manners puzzled and oppressed him. He feared that he was not acquiring the social graces which meant so much to him as quickly and readily as he would have liked. If only Elise were there to counsel him and help him to avoid repeating the blunders he felt but did not really know he had made. There is an air of sour grapes about his denunciation of the empty life and silly ambitions of the personages who lived in court circles.

Hebbel was fortunate enough, however, to gain admission to

other circles in which he felt much more at home, namely the household and friends of the well-known Danish writer Adam Oehlenschläger (1779-1850), who prided himself on occupying a place in both German and Danish literature. Oehlenschläger's enthusiasm for Nordic and Germanic culture had been brought to a high pitch by his contact with the Norwegian Henrik Steffens (1773-1845), whose lectures on German letters had a revolutionary effect throughout Scandinavia, not least on Oehlenschläger. The latter's claim to a position in German literature rested upon the fact that he wrote some of his works, notably the tragedy *Correggio,* in German. It was thus a great piece of good fortune for Hebbel that he won the favor of this very influential man of letters. Their association was very cordial, and the melancholy German was often astounded by the antics of the whimsical Dane.

Hebbel was no less astounded by the eccentricity of the world-renowned sculptor, Bertel Thorvaldsen (1768-1844), whom he visited in his studio, and whose works, neo-classic though they were, he greatly admired. He admired no less Thorvaldsen's courage and perseverance and felt a certain kinship with this man whose start in life had been only little more auspicious than Hebbel's own. From Thorvaldsen he gained fresh insight into one of the arts, but from Oehlenschläger he received great practical help, for Oehlenschläger, who knew the right people, urged Hebbel to apply for a travel stipend rather than for a license to teach at the University of Kiel, and composed a letter recommending Hebbel most warmly to the King.

Hebbel now requested a second audience with Christian VIII. The request was granted, and on January 23, 1843, Hebbel appeared again before His Majesty. Oehlenschläger's letter had the desired effect; the King promised his support, and Hebbel did not take his leave until Christian had signified that the audience was over.

There now came a period of waiting for official notification of the award. These were anxious days for Hebbel, for something could conceivably go wrong, he thought, if, for example, he failed to recognize and pay his respects to some of the influential persons whom he might chance to meet while out walking; and he resolved that, if he should receive the stipend he sought, he would certainly apply part of it to learning proper social behavior (letters to Elise, February 5 and 27, 1843). The risk of giving offense through ignorance of the mysteries of etiquette soon became rather remote, for during the first week in March he suffered an attack of "rheumatism," which eventually confined him to his bed and caused him great suffering. Whether it was really rheumatism or a preliminary bout of the illness to which he eventually succumbed is uncertain. It is less uncertain that the disease, whatever it was, was the result of his long history of self-privation. In Copenhagen he lived on bread and coffee, as was his wont when away from Elise; and he kept his room unheated during the cold and damp Danish winter, depending on the library of Christiansborg Castle or the rooms of the "Atheneum" reading circle for warmth as well as books.

Ironically, all of Hebbel's savings were wiped out by the expenses incurred by his illness, and he was close to despair. But now, even more than earlier, Oehlenschläger proved himself a true friend, for he came to see Hebbel regularly, spending several hours a day with him, reading to him, and talking about literary matters. And then, on April 4, Oehlenschläger brought him the great news: he had learned that the King had granted Hebbel a travel stipend of 600 Reichstaler (Danish) per year for two years. They both wept tears of joy. Now it was only a matter of waiting for the official confirmation. Gradually the rheumatism began to ease up, more the result of mild spring weather than the effect of the great news, but the two together rekindled Hebbel's optimism. The last two weeks of his stay in Copenhagen were filled with making plans for the future, making courtesy calls on the various notables who had helped him and who might be helpful again when he applied for an extension of his stipend, and chafing that his rheumatism still handicapped him. Finally, on the evening of April 27, 1843, he set out on the return journey to Hamburg. Elise was there to meet him when he arrived.

CHAPTER 5

The Breakthrough

I *The First Masterpiece*

THE next four months were largely unproductive. To be sure, on May 1 Hebbel was able to record in his journal that he had completed the first act of his middle-class tragedy, i.e., *Maria Magdalene*, which he had conceived in Munich and begun in Copenhagen on March 10. But the play was not finished until December 4 in Paris. Just what made this summer so barren is doubtful. Hebbel writes of an illness, perhaps a partial relapse, that confined him to his quarters, and there are in the diaries some unexplained references to the pangs of love. Another diary entry mentions that his little son fell and struck his head so hard that he bled from the nose, but nothing more is said about this. On August 29 Hebbel records that he had seen Emma Schröder again: "It was not without sadness, for this girl, the finest I have ever known, years ago was drawn to me in love, and if contemptible things had not interposed themselves between her and me, I too would have tasted the greatest happiness earth has to give, and that might perhaps have refreshed my life in its innermost root." It was a great consolation to him, he felt, that Emma had had a conversation with Elise and explained how she had been defamed by an envious old woman.

The only literary production of this summer worthy of note was an essay, "Mein Wort über das Drama," which was a polemical reply to an unfriendly article about *Judith* written by Johan Ludvig Heiberg (1791-1860). Heiberg was one of the most influential figures in contemporary literary circles in Denmark, a philosopher, critic, and creative writer. He was stimulated to attack Hebbel by reading a translation into Danish of a brief essay by Hebbel entitled "Ein Wort über das Drama." On the basis of this essay and the stage-version of *Judith*, Heiberg wrote that Hebbel was guilty of confusing his concepts and of abstracting life from the objective forces which determine it, with the result that his drama presented mere individuals detached from the eternal principle. It was awkward that the attack on Hebbel by the foremost literary authority in Denmark should so nearly coincide with the award of a travel grant by the Danish King. Therefore, Hebbel says, he was compelled to take up the cudgels against Heiberg.

He did this by reprinting "Ein Wort über das Drama" as the introduction to the body of the new essay "Mein Wort über das Drama," in which he first pointed out what he considered Heiberg's misinterpretations. He was particularly indignant that Heiberg had based his criticism on the acting version of *Judith*, which was admittedly a compromise with the theater director's demands. After taking up various points, he reiterated his basic ideas, with some of which we are already familiar:

Art and philosophy have one and the same task, but they seek to perform it in different ways. If philosophy strives to comprehend the Idea [the basic metaphysical principle, the All or Absolute] immediately, art contents itself with annihilating everything that contradicts it in the world of phenomena. Philosophy has not yet been adequate to its part of the common task, it has drawn the periphery closer and closer to the mysterious center; but the leap from the periphery into the center has not yet been successful, for individuation has not yet been reduced to its intrinsic necessity. Art, on the other hand, has always fulfilled its function in due season among the Ancients and the Moderns, it has always been able to resolve individuation by means of the excess implanted in it, and to free the Idea from its imperfect form. [That is to say, the mere existence of the individual is an excess, a challenge to the Idea and an imperfection in it.] Guilt lies in the excess, but so also, insofar as there can be a question of reconciliation in the sphere of art, does reconciliation, for the individual constitutes an excess only because, being incomplete, it has no claim to permanence and thus must work towards its own destruction. This guilt is aboriginal, cannot be divorced from the concept of man, and scarcely enters his consciousness: it is posited with life itself. As the darkest of threads it runs through the traditions of all peoples, and original sin itself is nothing more than a consequence derived from it and modified by Christianity. It does not depend upon the direction of human will, it is involved in all human action, whether we pursue good or evil: we can exceed the bounds in the one way as well as in the other. The loftiest drama is concerned with nothing else, and it is not merely a matter of indifference whether the hero perishes in a praiseworthy or reprehensible endeavor, but, if the most devastating portrayal is to be effected it is essential that it be in a praiseworthy endeavor. . . . Drama, as I construct it, does not by any means end with a dissonance, for it causes the dualistic form of being to resolve itself [that is, to cancel itself out]. If I may use an image: it represents two circles on the water, which, precisely by encroaching upon each other, destroy themselves and dissolve into a single large circle that smoothes the ruffled surface for the image of the sun. But by accepting individuation as an immediately given fact without seeking the *causa prima*, regardless of the question of creation, drama does, to be sure, leave one dissonance unresolved, and that is the original dissonance, which it neglected from the very first. It does not, therefore, leave guilt unatoned, but it leaves the intrinsic cause of guilt unrevealed. But this is the direction in which drama vanishes into one and the same night with the riddle of the cosmos. The utmost it attains is the satisfaction it procures for the Idea through the destruction of the individual that opposes the Idea by his activity or by his mere existence. This is a satisfaction which may be incomplete, if the individual goes down sullen and defiant, and thus gives notice in advance that it will again emerge, struggling, at another point in the cosmos. Or it may be complete if the individual, in its very destruction, obtains a clarified view of its relation to the Whole and departs in peace. But this is only half enough even in the second instance, for even if the schism is healed, why did it have to occur? To this I have never found an answer, and no one will find it, who asks in all seriousness.

This, except for a partial explication of his views on the relation of drama to history, is the essential argument of Hebbel's reply to Professor Heiberg. Since he went into this matter in greater detail in another critical essay, the "Vorwort zu Maria Magdalene" (March, 1844), a discussion of these views may be deferred for the time being.

For a long time, Hebbel was undecided to what centers of culture he should travel, but finally he made up his mind to go to Paris. It is rather surprising that he was not impatient to be off, for his relations with Elise seem to have worsened. A diary entry for May 20 runs: "Human beings in their relationships with one another always think only of their conscious will and actions, when they accuse each other of lessening affection. But they never think of the stage of development which they have attained without knowing it, or to which they have fallen back, and which is often in the most glaring contradiction to an earlier stage." Whatever the changes that were taking place in his consciousness or subconsciousness, he waited until September 9 before leaving Hamburg for Le Havre. Although neither Hebbel nor Elise could have known it with any certainty, they were destined never to be reunited in the old way.

When he had made up his mind to go to Paris, Hebbel began to study French but had no greater success with that language than he had had earlier with Latin. Despite this handicap, he reached Paris without mishap thanks to the good offices of a German Russian who was competent in French. Hebbel did not, however, stay in Paris, but went on to St. Germain-en-Laye, where a Hamburg acquaintance had urged him to take lodgings. This turned out to be a great mistake, for all the monuments of culture and history that he wanted to see were almost inaccessible to him unless he was ready to spend money on transportation, and this, of course, he was not ready to do. Eventually, in mid-October, he moved into new lodgings in Paris.

Meanwhile he had made some acquaintances, notably Heinrich Heine and Felix Bamberg. With Heine—although, as he said, he could talk with him about the most profound subjects—relations were and remained a little uncertain, but Bamberg became one of a considerable number of men who idolized Hebbel and put themselves at his service. Soon after meeting Hebbel and reading his *Judith,* Bamberg fell under his spell, took him walking in Paris, and became not only his guide but also his sounding board, for Hebbel was now at work again on his middle-class tragedy, *Maria Magdalene.* It was supposedly Bamberg who urged him to write a foreword to that play in order to clarify his esthetic theories.

Shortly afterwards Hebbel moved into his new quarters in Paris, and in the midst of work on his play he heard from Elise that their son Max had died and that Elise was pregnant again. The shock was great. To be sure, he had heard already that Max was ill, but he had not paid great attention to the news, and he seems not to have taken the possibility of another pregnancy very seriously. So much the greater was his sense of guilt, and he reproached himself bitterly for having been indifferent to the child. "Rarely had I any other thought," he wrote

in his diary for October 24, "than this: 'How shall I feed him?'
And in my unmanly despondency I was dull and apathetic to
the happiness which surrounded me, which I needed only to
take into my arms in order to have a treasure for all time." The
impression left by the entire entry, which is quite long, is that of
a mixture of sincerity and posing, as if the writer enjoyed plung-
ing himself into grief, which gave him material for his journal.
And, indeed, he makes this admission in a letter to Elise, dated
November 6: "There is a sensual pleasure in destroying one-
self, in tearing open the wounds when they begin to heal, and
to let the noblest life-blood pour forth as an offering to the
dead. I know this pleasure and have often sinned in this way."

In his letters to Elise, however, Hebbel was much more re-
strained and calm than in his diary, deliberately so, because
he feared what might happen to her or what she might do to
herself. Repeatedly he begged her not to take foot-baths,
which, it must be inferred, she threatened to do as a means of
producing an abortion, and he vowed that the thought of the
second child filled him with joy. Moreover, in his very first
letter after receiving the news (October 23) he spoke of their
marriage as a settled question and debated how they could
most speedily be united. The next two letters, dated October
25 and 31, show Hebbel somewhat less eager for a reunion, but
the letter of November 6 is full of facts and figures demonstrat-
ing the difficulty and impracticality either of Elise's coming to
Paris or his returning to Hamburg. Succeeding letters attempted to console Elise in one way or another. The culmination
of these attempts was a poem entitled "Maximilian Friedrich
Hebbel an seine Mutter." In this poem, the deceased child
speaks to his mother through Hebbel and explains that in death
will be found the answer to the great cosmic riddle: What is
the necessity of the dualism, why the One and the Many? It
is scarcely surprising that Elise found little comfort in the abstract speculations of the poem. Hebbel notes in his diary for
January 19, 1844: "I had expected some lasting effect from my
letters and my profound poem in *terza rima*, but in spite of her
words I see that all this does no good. It is as though somebody
tried to patch up a cabin for her after the end of the world."

Through all the distress and turmoil Hebbel had continued
working on *Maria Magdalene* and had managed to finish it on

December 4, 1843. The foreword to the play was written three months later.

In this foreword, Hebbel begins with the proposition that the drama, being the loftiest of all the arts, has the task of representing the human and social condition in its relation to the Idea. This relation is revealed best in times of stress. True drama, the highest drama, is therefore possible only when a decisive change in the world is taking place. So far in the history of the drama, there have been two such critical moments. The first was in ancient Greece, when paganism had become an outworn creed and the drama exposed the "nerve of the Idea running through all the variegated divinities of Olympus," namely Fate. For this reason, the individual was shown as being powerless in his opposition to the moral forces. The second time was in the emerging Protestant world of Elizabethan England when Shakespeare's drama emancipated the individual through the terrible dialectic of his characters, who, so far as they were men of action, eliminated every living being about them, or, so far as they were men of ideas, such as Hamlet, would banish God from the world by means of the boldest and most terrifying questions.

If Shakespearean drama put the dialectic into the individual, the next stage in this logical development must put the dialectic into the Idea, and Goethe pointed the way in this direction in his *Faust* and also in the *Wahlverwandtschaften* (ELECTIVE AFFINITIES). To examine and analyze the Idea so as to reveal the aboriginal dualism is the main task of modern philosophy and art, a task which, Hebbel suggests, it has been left for him to perform. The examination of the Idea must be undertaken, not with the hope of changing it, for that is impossible, but with the hope of establishing morality on a true metaphysical basis. In this way, dramatic art must be in keeping with the spirit of the age, for nineteenth-century man does not want new and unparalleled institutions, but a better foundation for those already existing; he wants them to be supported only by morality and necessity, which are identical. This new play, *Maria Magdalene,* is completely contemporary, not only in setting and costume, but also in its revelation of the crisis in the contemporary form of the Idea. Whereas earlier middle-class tragedies were based on accidents of a given situation and thus really no tragedies at all since the disaster could always be averted if the situation were altered, Hebbel maintains that his tragedy of the middle-class grows out of the very nature of the middle-class and is therefore truly inevitable.

The sense of inevitability in *Maria Magdalene* is one of Hebbel's very great achievements, a demonstration that he had reached maturity as a playwright and that he had attained mastery of his craft. In this play, he makes superb use of the technique of construction known as the analytic exposition, the same technique that is employed in *Oedipus Rex* and in Heinrich von Kleist's comedy *Der zerbrochene Krug*. That is, the dominating events have already taken place when the curtain rises, and the action seen on the stage flows from these events as it reveals what they were. Thus, as each character learns a part of the truth about the past, he is impelled to take certain actions, which, in their turn, lead to further revelations, and so on until the tragedy is complete. It is as though we were witnessing an intricate dance, every step of which it is natural and necessary for each character to take at just the time he takes it.

Despite the title, the central figure of the play, and, in a sense, its hero, is Meister Anton, a cabinet-maker, who lives in a small town somewhere in Hebbel's Germany.[1] He is the model of lower middle-class respectability and honesty, an honesty so extreme that it is said of him that if by chance one letter too many were carved on his tombstone, his ghost would find no rest until the letter were removed. Severe as he is with himself, he is no less severe and demanding in his relations with all those whom he does not consider respectable. Thus, when he was drinking beer in the tavern, an officer of the law put his mug down beside Meister Anton's as though proposing that they drink together. Meister Anton sharply rebuffed the man, saying that in former times he would not have been allowed inside the tavern with decent folk. As a consequence, the officer conceives an implacable hatred of Meister Anton and is determined to have his revenge.

Anton has thus created a situation which is potentially dangerous to him. He has created an equally dangerous situation in his own household. His wife, for all her docility and readiness to accept her husband's word as law, has spoiled and pampered their son Karl until he has become selfish and thoughtless, and has incurred gambling debts. Karl's need for diversion, his frivolous habits, however, can be explained as a reaction against the domestic tyranny of his father, which the latter has imposed because he is convinced that his moral duty prescribes such tyranny. In all its details his household is governed by specific regulations, which to Karl seem trivial and insufferable, but which are part of Anton's moral code. "The hat belongs on the third hook, not the fourth, at nine-thirty it is time to be tired, before Martinmas no freezing, after Martinmas no sweating, thou shalt love and fear God"—thus Karl characterizes the multiple commandments of the household, from which he longs to escape by going to sea. The excessive rigidity of Meister Anton's world, however, has not come about because Meister Anton takes pleasure in inflicting pain upon himself or others. He has developed all this grim discipline as a protection. As he says to Leonhard, who has just asked permission to marry his daughter Klara: "I wasn't born a prickly hedge-hog any more than you were, but gradually I turned into one. At first all my quills were turned in upon me. Then everybody pinched and squeezed my soft smooth skin, and they were all delighted when I shrank back because the sharp ends stuck into my heart and inwards. But I didn't care for this. I reversed my skin so they pricked their fingers on the quills, and then they left me alone."

Anton's defenses are not completely effective, however, for tears still come to his eyes when he thinks of Meister Gebhard, the man who took him in as an apprentice when his father had died and the widow and her little son were in desperate circumstances. Gebhard not only made young Anton his apprentice and taught him his trade without asking for compensation, but he gave him board and lodging and occasionally sent him home with half a ham for his mother, cautioning the boy to conceal the gift from his wife. Later, when Anton had established himself, he went to make a friendly call on Meister Gebhard and found him, desperate and confused, in the act of cutting his throat. Anton saved his master's life but was able to rescue him from financial ruin only by lending him the thousand Taler he had saved for Klara's dowry. Since Meister Gebhard died without being able to repay the money, Anton's admirable act jeopardized Klara's future, for Leonhard was more interested in her dowry than her person. Thus, on the one hand, Meister Anton's kindness of heart has put him and his family at the mercy of that society which his gruffness was intended to repulse, and on the other hand, the gruff and bitter manner has by no means made him independent of society, but has actually made him more subservient. He drives himself and his family to conform to the minutiae of middle-class conventions in order not to be the object of pity or scorn. The one thing which he cannot endure is to be disgraced, dishonored in the eyes of his own middle class.

Undoubtedly, the most terrible thing that could happen to Meister Anton would be for members of his family to bring disgrace upon him through dishonesty or indecency. He is promptly dishonored in both ways. His son Karl is unjustly imprisoned on the charge of stealing money from an article of furniture he was polishing, and his daughter Klara yields to the demands of her fiancé (whom she does not love) to prove to him in the only way he cannot doubt that she seriously intends to go through with the marriage.

To understand how Klara, who is not at all rebellious like Karl and who is bound to her father with strong ties of love and affection, could so transgress against the moral code, it is necessary to go back to her early youth when she fell in love with a young man named Friedrich, who returned her love honestly and openly. But Friedrich apparently removed himself from lower-middle-class circles by becoming a university student. And during his years at the university he seemed to forget Klara. He ceased to write to her, and her family and her friends urged her to forget him in turn, ridiculing her for supposing that he still thought of her. Her mother's advice to marry within her class and her praise of Leonhard had its strong effect also.

The pressure of opinion and her own wounded pride thus gradually pushed Klara into the engagement with Leonhard. Then Friedrich came back to his home town to take the post of secretary, and the old feelings awoke. But now Klara was engaged to Leonhard, who feared the revival of the love Klara and Friedrich once felt for each other. Thus, when Leonhard went with Klara to a dance at which it became apparent that his fear was justified, he took prompt steps to make sure that he would not lose his most precious possession, namely Klara and her dowry. Klara also recognized that she and Friedrich were strongly attracted to each other and, precisely because she was her father's daughter and felt that her word was sacred, recognized Leonhard's claim upon her, and the supposed truth of his assertion that she would be risking nothing if she took the engagement seriously. And so, from a combination of motives, and in order to prove to herself that she honored her word, as well as to fight down the rekindling flame of love for Friedrich, she gave herself to Leonhard.

Now, after a two-week interval during which Leonhard has not come to call on Klara, he suddenly appears before her one Sunday morning when he knows that she will be at home to prepare the midday meal. Her mother, barely recovered from a dangerous illness, has gone to church to offer thanks for her recovery, as has Meister Anton. Karl has left the house also. Leonhard has come to tell Klara that the last obstacle to their marriage has been removed, for he has obtained the post of cashier. If Leonhard has hitherto seemed only tolerably unpleasant to Klara, he now reveals himself as someone she can only loathe and despise. He has obtained the post of cashier with the help of some comrades who induced his competitor to drink more than he could tolerate just before coming to the public examination. The reason he has not called on Klara for two weeks is that he has been paying court to the burgomaster's hump-backed niece in order to have her speak a good word for him to her uncle who dotes on her. In order to do this he trumped up a quarrel with Klara so that he could stay away without exciting comment. Klara, full of horror and dismay, goes to the kitchen to prepare the midday meal, leaving Leonhard alone until Meister Anton comes. Anton is bitter because Karl has broken his promise to go to church and give thanks for his mother's recovery. After a while, Leonhard asks formally for Klara's hand in marriage, even though Anton has just told him in jest, as Leonhard thinks, that he has lost Klara's dowry.

Leonhard's answer to this disclosure is seemingly so resolute and manly that Anton tells him what has become of the money— a bitter blow for Leonhard, but not sufficient grounds for breaking off the engagement. Klara's mother comes home, and while she and Anton are talking, Leonhard finds an item in the newspaper which he reads aloud: some jewels have been stolen from the desk in the house of Wolfram the merchant. Meister Anton's first thought is that Karl had been polishing that desk.

The Breakthrough

During the ensuing conversation, the law officer Adam, Meister Anton's enemy, comes to arrest Karl on the charge of theft. The mother drops dead of shock as Adam savors his revenge, ransacking the house as brutally as possible. Leonhard now sees his way out of his engagement with the penniless Klara, hurries away, and speedily sends a maid with the formal notice that a man in his position cannot marry the sister of a thief. When Meister Anton tells Klara to let him go and she automatically replies, "I cannot!" he suspects the truth and demands that Klara swear to him that she "is as she is supposed to be." Klara replies, "I swear to you that I will never bring disgrace upon you."

And so, after the burial of Klara's mother, life goes on for a while in Meister Anton's house, Klara's anxiety growing and Anton's dreadful suspicion becoming more intense as he writhes at the thought that his son is a thief. And he says to Klara: "If you become a woman such as your mother was, people will say it was not the parents' fault that the boy went astray, for the daughter is walking the strait and narrow path as an example for all. And I intend to do my part, I will make it easier for you than it is for others. The moment I notice that people are pointing their fingers at you too, I will shave, and then, this I swear to you, I will shave away the whole man. . . . I cannot live in a world where people would have to feel pity for me, if they were not to spit at the sight of me. . . . I can endure everything and I have proved it, but not disgrace. Pile anything you want on my back, only do not cut the nerve that holds me together."

Meister Anton leaves to do business with the lumber-dealer, and no sooner has he gone than Wolfram arrives and tells Klara that the lost jewels have been found and that Karl's name is cleared. Immediately after Wolfram's departure, Friedrich comes, ostensibly to bring the same news, but actually to see whether Klara is content with Leonhard as her choice. When he asks her whether she loves Leonhard, she cries out, "It's you I love!" Friedrich, overjoyed, proposes speedy marriage, but Klara tells him that she has no choice but to implore Leonhard to marry her. Friedrich, now comprehending the situation, exclaims, "No man can get over that!" For Klara this means the end of the rising hope that perhaps someone would show her mercy, and she goes to Leonhard to beg him to marry her, now that it can no longer be said that she is the sister of a thief. Leonhard, however, blandly refuses, saying that he has committed himself to marriage with the burgomaster's niece, and Klara, who sees no way out except suicide, returns to her home to make it look as though she had met an accidental death by drowning. Friedrich compels Leonhard to fight a duel with him in order to kill the only man who could point the finger of shame at Klara. He does, indeed, kill Leonhard, but he is himself mortally wounded.

Friedrich manages to make his way back to Klara's house, where he finds Karl and Meister Anton. Friedrich's appearance arouses Karl's suspicion that something has happened to Klara and he runs out to the well from which she had said she was going to get some fresh water for him. Friedrich tries to make Anton swear not to cast off his daughter under any circumstances, but Anton refuses and even finds it in his heart to approve the desperate measure by which Klara tried to avert disgrace. It was a futile measure, however, for someone saw that Klara jumped rather than stumbled into the well. Meister Anton's comment is, "She has spared me nothing." Friedrich, who has realized too late that he should have opened his arms to Klara rather than let himself be governed by what a scoundrel like Leonhard knew and might say, replies to Anton, "She did what she could, you did not deserve to have her act succeed." But Anton, unbroken to the end, counters, "Or she did not," and remains alone, sunk in thoughts, saying, "I no longer understand the world."

It will be recalled that in the "Foreword to Maria Magdalene" Hebbel maintained that the highest drama is possible when a decisive change is taking place in the world, when the prevailing form of the Idea, through dialectic change, is being counterbalanced and eventually, perhaps, replaced by a new form. The first such historical crisis took place in ancient Greece, when the first phase of the dialectic process subordinated the individual to the prevailing form of the Idea, namely Fate. In the second phase, in Shakespeare's drama, the dialectic process ran its course in the individuals. In the third phase, in Hebbel's Europe and in his drama, the dialectic is within the Idea itself, that is, within the prevailing form of the Idea. In *Maria Magdalene*, the prevailing form is social structure shaped by middle-class ethics.

All the characters of the play belong to the lower middle class and most of them unquestioningly accept its standards of values and behavior. Except for Friedrich and Karl they so closely identify themselves with their society that they do not seriously question its dictates. As Hebbel wrote to Mme. Stich-Crelinger (December 11, 1843), "the tragedy is derived very simply from the middle-class world itself, from its obstinate and self-sufficient adherence to traditional patriarchal beliefs and from its inability to accommodate itself to complicated situations." Just as Genoveva was the representative of God on earth, so is Meister Anton the individual embodiment of the Idea, the moral code personified, and yet its victim, as all the others are victims. His wife, of course, obeys her husband in everything, except that she tries to shield Karl and makes excuses for him. And even Karl, although he rebels against Meister Anton and his commandments so far as they affect him, has no thought of trying to overthrow the system. "When Father isn't here, your brother is your guardian," he says to Klara, as he snatches Leonhard's letter out of her hand. And Klara herself is the nearly perfect product of her society, docile, self-sacrificing, honest.

Indeed, it is her personal integrity, the ideal and the essence of her code and Meister Anton's, which brings about her downfall: she consents to Leonhard's demand in order to prove her honesty to him and to herself. And it is her personal integrity which makes it impossible for her to take the only way out of her tragic situation, to marry Friedrich, concealing her condition from him until later. If she could thus have secured the appearance of legitimacy, she could have saved both her father and herself, at least, her outward self. But this is impossible to her, for she does not merely acquiesce in the standards of her code, she lives them.[2] As for Friedrich, although he has had experiences which may have served to give him a somewhat broader perspective, at the moment when he utters the fateful words, "No man can get over that," his words and feelings are dictated by the conventional standards of his time and place. Even the base Leonhard is not immoral in the sense of being at odds with his society: his whole endeavor is to conform to the demands of that society and obtain an honored although not necessarily honorable place in it. The spectacle thus presented is that of a human condition that is crumbling through the logic of its inner development; or, in Hebbel's abstract language, the dialectic has been put into the Idea. The fact that Meister Anton destroys his own world shows that the form of the Idea which is personified in him is ripe for change, that the structure must be altered if there is to be room for individuals within it; and since the One lives and moves by virtue of the many who momentarily escape from it, room must be made for the individuals in order that the world may continue to exist. And that, for Hebbel, is the only necessity there is. What happens to the individuals is of no moment.

When the play was completed, Hebbel, thinking of the good reception accorded to his *Judith* in Berlin, sent the manuscript there, but not even the good offices of Mme. Stich-Crelinger could prevail upon the management to accept the play for production. The reason given was that it was not proper to show a pregnant woman on the stage. Hebbel, of course, cited the examples of Klärchen in Goethe's *Egmont* and Gretchen in *Faust,* but to no avail. Hebbel's first true masterpiece came before the public first in printed form (1844). Not until March 13, 1846 was it performed, and then in far-off Königsberg.

II *Domestic Happiness and Financial Security*

Hebbel remained in Paris some little time after the publication of *Maria Magdalene,* still beset by troubles and worries about his future. Elise, of course, wished to marry, and Hebbel, despite his aversion, felt the legitimacy of her wish. But he was strengthened in his resolution not to return to Hamburg at this time by the realization that a request for a renewal of his travel stipend would certainly be refused if he addressed it to the King from Hamburg. Oehlenschläger, to whom he had confided his problems, confirmed his feeling and pointed out that marriage without income to maintain a household would solve nothing. Another concern that weighed upon Hebbel at this time was that he had nothing to show for having attended a university, for neither Heidelberg nor Munich would grant him a degree. He therefore more or less bought a doctorate from the University of Erlangen, which at that time handed out diplomas on the basis of a written dissertation and the payment of a fee. Hebbel, unfortunately, did not have enough money to claim his diploma, but he made use of the title anyway. The self-made doctor was, however, becoming impatient to move on, feeling that Paris, for all its notorious gaiety, could offer him nothing more, and he left for Rome on September 26, 1844.

Rome, where he arrived on October 3, turned out to be rather uncongenial. Since he could not learn Italian any more readily than French, he had very little direct contact with the Romans, but associated largely with a group of German and Austrian painters, with whom he had long discourses on art. Through associating with them, and merely through everyday living, he became familiar with sculpture and painting, arts which previously had no especial significance for him. His acquaintance with Thorvaldsen and his sculptures had been too isolated an experience, and he had scarcely assimilated what he had learned. But now Thorvaldsen's art was put into perspective as he saw Michelangelo's mighty works and, especially, the statues of antiquity. Parenthetically it might be said here that his taste and judgments were thoroughly conventional: Greek and Roman sculpture he regarded as the summit, Michelangelo was the greatest of the moderns. This constitutes a definite parallel to his evaluation of the Greek dramatists and Shakespeare, even though the plastic arts never meant as much to him as did literature. Perhaps the greatest gain he derived from his stay in Italy, especially Naples, was a certain relaxation, a more immediate and sensuous enjoyment of nature. In Naples he was also greatly impressed by the great gulf separating the very rich from the abjectly poor. This was an observation which he was to make use of in his *Trauerspiel in Sizilien*.

It must not, however, be supposed that his life in Italy, because of his association with the rather light-hearted artists and his participation in such festivals as the Roman Carnival, was on the whole gay and sunny. All his anxieties, doubts, fears had come with him. In 1845 he was nearing the end of the time provided for by his travel stipend, and he applied for a year's extension. This request, however, was refused. Instead, he received a grant of merely two hundred Taler to defray the expenses of his return to Hamburg. This was, of course, a great disappointment to him, especially since he might have more or less inadvertently been the cause. It seemed at least possible that Hebbel had offended the Danish King by failing to hold up the publication of *Maria Magdalene* with its dedication to Christian VIII until receiving His Majesty's consent. This explanation was not implausible in view of the nature of the play. Whatever the explanation, the fact remained that Hebbel was again in straitened circumstances and, because he had not been able to do creative work since the completion of *Maria Magdalene*, terrified that he might have written himself out. To these worries was added Elise's growing insistence that they marry.

When Hebbel had received the news of his son's death and of Elise's second pregnancy, he had, as we know, committed himself to marrying and might possibly have honored his commitment had Elise come to Paris or had he gone to Hamburg. Elise took his letters and his promises very seriously and began to sign herself as his wife, or, as was the case in negotiating with the Danish officials, as his fiancée. Hebbel was furious and upbraided her vehemently for this act which would plunge them both into further complications and embarrassments. She should have understood, he wrote on December 16, 1844, that his assurances of his wish to marry her were meant not as serious promises but as words of sympathy and comfort merely. "How can you believe," he asks her, "that I look upon one child differently from the other? For me a child is a promissory note which I cannot pay, nothing more. And a marriage which has no substantial foundation in property is a leap into an abyss."

When Elise persisted in her efforts to make him irrevocably commit himself to her, he pointed out that everyone "must strive to realize the condition of his existence, and for a woman this condition is the possession of the man she loves.—It makes absolutely no sense—if on the one hand you urge marriage and on the other you say that you wish nothing for yourself.—Love is completely egotistic, and the only reason this ordinarily is not felt is that the egotism of the one coincides with the egotism of the other." And so Elise's pleas had only the effect of strengthening his resolution not to marry her, however much he might admire her nobility of soul. This resolution was expressed unequivocally in his diary entry of February 21, 1845: "Shake off everything that hampers you in your development, even if it were a human being that loves you; for what destroys you cannot benefit another."

And so the time approached when the exhaustion of his very carefully budgeted resources made it necessary to leave Italy. In fact, he had to borrow a hundred Taler from the painter Ludwig Gurlitt, who had become one of his close friends. On October 29, 1845, he left Rome, bound for Vienna and Berlin, and resolved not to return to Hamburg to live. As things turned out, he did not get beyond Vienna, for in Vienna love, fortune, and success awaited him.

The change for the better began to make itself felt even on the way to Vienna. On the journey, he had made several acquaintances, including a young Polish count who lived in Vienna and helped him to find suitable lodgings. As soon as he was established he called on Regierungsrat Deinhardstein, the editor of the *Wiener Jahrbücher,* who had reviewed his works favorably. Deinhardstein encouraged Hebbel to call on Count Moritz Dietrichstein, director of the court theater. Here Hebbel experienced a bitterly felt disappointment, for Dietrichstein had apparently never heard of *Judith, Genoveva,* or *Maria Magdalene,* and a call on Franz Grillparzer, the great Viennese playwright, was of no service in getting the plays performed.[3] Weary and depressed, Hebbel prepared to leave Vienna.

And then a sort of miracle occurred. On the way to make arrangements to leave, he met someone he knew only very slightly who told him that there were two Galician barons in the city who were eager to make his acquaintance. Hebbel abruptly changed his plans and proposed a meeting with the barons the very same day. But when he got to the appointed place, he found an invitation to spend the evening with the noblemen in their hotel. What ensued must have been one of Hebbel's most delightful triumphs, a fine banquet followed by a night of revelry, with toasts in champagne, recitations of passages from Hebbel's plays, apostrophes to his genius. The two noblemen were Wilhelm and Julius Zerboni di Sposetti, who had long been ardent admirers of *Judith.* They had learned of Hebbel's presence in Vienna from the Polish count, Hebbel's fellow passenger, and had promptly resolved to honor the poet whom they so greatly admired. But they were not content with a single, although glorious, celebration. They showered him with invitations to dine. They made him their guest at the hotel. In a word, through their efforts Hebbel became a literary lion to whom the fashionable salons of Vienna were opened. The brick-layer's son began to mount the ladder that led to the peak of social distinction. But, more than this, to the Zerbonis Hebbel owed, indirectly, the greatest happiness and good fortune of his life: marriage with the woman who made it possible for him to write his greatest plays and achieve distinction such as he could only have dreamed of, but not hoped for.

One evening, at the meeting of a literary society, the poet Otto Prechtler told Hebbel that the actress Christine Enghaus had long been eager to act the role of Judith. Hebbel quite naturally asked to be introduced and was, apparently, greatly impressed, and so was Christine. When he took his leave, saying that he could not remain much longer in Vienna, she had, so she wrote much later in a letter to Emil Kuh,[4] a sense of sadness and compassion: "I had heard of his poverty. His wretched clothing, the black dress-coat which did not fit him, bore eloquent testimony to it. 'If I were rich,' I said to myself, 'I would provide a carefree future for him.'" Christine's sense of sadness, however, soon changed into something else, for Hebbel did not leave Vienna as he had planned. "I believed that he had left long before," she writes, "and then one day he stood at my door again, but as though he had been ennobled, that is, outwardly: a fine elegant overcoat, and hat, gloves—I could scarcely believe my eyes." This time also Hebbel left the impression that he would soon leave Vienna, and Christine was, if anything, sadder than before. But a week later Hebbel was back, declaring that it was she who kept him from leaving, and asking permission to call more often. The next time they met they became engaged. They were married on May 26, 1846.

The self-confidence and courage required to pay court to the popular and impressive actress Hebbel owed in some measure to the Zerbonis, for it was they who had given him the elegant clothing, presenting it to him as a Christmas surprise. And it was they, of course, who gave him the opportunity to polish and show off the social accomplishments which he felt he had acquired. In a letter to Elise dated December 18, 1845, he writes: "My travels have, as I am just finding out, brought me a great and inestimable gain: I have learned proper social behavior, something I did not know formerly. And how could I have learned it in the solitude to which I condemned myself? It was very comfortable to take my ease on your sofa. I was protected against all the biting gusts of wind, but to balance that I caught cold as soon as I stepped outside. This secluded mode of life was most unnatural for a person like myself, who needs to talk in order to feel expansive. It's a good thing for me that traveling pulled me out of myself." And he gives examples of sharp and witty replies he has made on various occasions.

This letter, and some of those immediately preceding it, are so boastful and condescending, so cold and distant, that Elise must have felt extremely apprehensive upon reading them. And when Hebbel wrote with affected casualness about the interest which the great actress had in *Judith,* Elise suspected the worst, and with the same affected casualness repeated some ugly gossip about Christine which had come to her ears from the time when the actress had been a member of the Hamburg theater. Hebbel, as he revealed in a letter to Felix Bamberg on June 27, 1846,[5] immediately wrote Elise a letter in which he informed her of his resolution to marry Christine. Although, he says, Elise had often assured him that he must not feel tied to her and was free to marry someone else if such a marriage would bring him happiness, now she behaved in such a way that her actions had not the

remotest resemblance to her assurances, nor did they comport with dignified acquiescence to necessity. Entangling herself in the most wretched sophistries, she at first maintained it was not the event itself that wounded her, but the way in which I had told her of the event. Then she said that I had, of course, been free, but only in the eventuality that I could have become completely happy, and that I would certainly not become completely happy. Now, after the wedding, she stoops even to the coarsest insult and accounts it a great deed that she has not taken legal action against me, something that she could not do because of the content of her letters. She showers me with extracts from my letters, which understandably say something very different from the correspondence as a whole, and demands that I, who have been supporting her for years and burdened myself with debt in Italy for her sake, that I make legal depositions concerning my readiness to provide for my child. Of course, I feel myself inwardly much freer than I would have felt if she had behaved differently, but I will confess to you that this experience is very bitter, for I don't know whether I should say, "She is like that," or "The world is like that!"

[81]

Earlier in the letter, Hebbel defends his decision to marry.

Even in Rome I was firmly resolved to put my affair in Hamburg back on the simple basis of friendship, where it had always been for me, and I phrased my letters accordingly. I mention this in order to show you that it was not the overpowering impression made upon me by a woman I had become acquainted with which brought on the crisis—that could, indeed, have been open to censure. I shuddered at the idea of having to live out my life at the side of a woman whom I had never loved and who had always known this. I felt that she would inevitably make me unhappy and would herself inevitably become unhappy because of this, unhappier than she would become through the termination of an association, which, in her case to be sure, was rooted in the depths of her nature, but which she, with her perfect knowledge of my feelings, should never have sought, and which permanently excluded me from a healthy human existence. One may make any sacrifice except the sacrifice of a whole life, if this life has any purpose other than that of being brought to a close. Life maintains itself only by means of incentive. The most complete weariness is the consequence if incentive is lacking, and if it is replaced by the duty to avoid it. A woman who could see her husband fade away in her arms and could find a surrogate in the consciousness that she possessed him as she might possess any other thing, would not deserve the man's sacrifice, and another woman would not demand such a sacrifice. There is no alternative.

Whether or not Hebbel's account of his break with Elise is literally true, we may suppose that the terrible shock and disappointment probably did cause Elise to show the worst side of her personality. The ugly gossip about Christine had a basis in fact: she had an illegitimate son, a circumstance that caused Hebbel considerable unhappiness and indecision. As he saw clearly, he was now involved in a real situation that resembled that of Klara and Friedrich in *Maria Magdalene*. He wrote to Bamberg in the letter already cited: "This very beautiful girl, whose nobility of heart is expressed in every word and every glance, I had not seen as many as three times when the full meaning of life, which only love can conjure up, was revealed to me again. I struggled with myself, whether I should flee, but not because of my affair in Hamburg, for this was over and done with for me, but because my new love imposed a bitter duty upon

[82]

me, a duty which I did not feel equal to any more than the Secretary in *Maria Magdalene*. Do you know why I did not flee? Because I am the author of this play, because I could not shirk the trial which fate put upon me without declaring my play and all my poetry to be despicable hypocrisy. Because I would have been ashamed, if in a representation of life I had expressed moral demands which were too hard for me to meet."

It must not be supposed, however, that Hebbel decided to ask Christine to marry him in order to demonstrate that he was superior to the middle-class standards which were revealed to be so oppressive in *Maria Magdalene*, although it is quite possible that this motive helped to influence him. Nor can it be assumed that he was carried off by an irresistible passion, although there is reason to believe that Hebbel and Christine were strongly attracted to each other. But perhaps predominant among the various motives which led Hebbel to marry was that with Christine's help he could fulfill what he felt to be his destiny. The diary entry for December 30 and 31, 1846, in which he resumes his old practice of viewing the year in retrospect, sheds a good deal of light on the matter:

I became engaged to Fräulein Enghaus. I did so surely out of love, but I would have sought to master this love and continued my journey, if the burden of life had not become so heavy upon me, that in the affection which this high-minded girl bestowed upon me I was compelled to see my only deliverance.—It is my feeling that after the age of thirty one can no longer appeal to irresistible passion, if he is not leading a completely empty life.—It is and will forever remain my conviction that the entire man is possessed by that power within him which is the most significant, for from it alone comes his own happiness and at the same time all the benefit which the world can get from him. In me this is the poetic power. How could I have kept it alive in my wretched struggle for existence, and how could I have continued to fight this fight, even poorly, without her?

Hebbel wrote this four days after the birth of his first child with Christine, a boy named Emil, whom they called Ariel. This son, Hebbel admitted, meant much more to him than Elise's children, and he contrasts his feelings of love for Emil with the coldness he felt for little Max, and now felt for the second child, Ernst, whom he had never seen. At the same time, however, he noted in the diary that nothing should deter him from fulfilling his duty toward the boy. It was not long before he was relieved of this duty, however, for Ernst, who had always been frail, died on May 12, 1847, almost three months to the day after the completely unexpected and terrifyingly swift death of Christine's son Emil, on February 14. Ernst had been ailing since birth, and Hebbel had been exchanging letters about his condition with Elise; that is, at least some parts of their letters, those parts which were not recriminatory, had been concerned with the child. It is clear from what has been preserved of these letters that Christine had suggested first that she and her husband might bring the child up in Vienna, where the climate was more healthful. Then, when it seemed that no amount of care could keep Ernst alive much longer, Christine suggested that Elise herself come to Vienna after the child's death. And finally, when news came that the boy was dead, it was at Christine's insistence that Hebbel urged Elise to come to stay with them.

This astounding invitation led to an even more astounding acceptance, an indication of Elise's desperate loneliness. She arrived in Vienna on May 29, 1847 and remained with the Hebbels as their guest until August 27, 1848. Despite the deep and genuine attachment of Hebbel and Christine, the household had never been serene. Soon after their marriage Hebbel instituted a new regimen. Christine's rather easy-going management and her generosity toward her kinfolk were abruptly stopped, for Hebbel insisted upon economy. Christine's income supported the household: whatever Hebbel managed to earn by his writings had to be used to support Elise and to cancel his debts to Gurlitt and the elder Rousseau. Christine's relatives, of course, resented being thus cut off, and, as a consequence, there were a good many unpleasant scenes, which Christine eventually learned to avoid by acquiescing in her husband's wishes.

Hebbel did not curb his hasty temper after Elise moved in with them, but flared up quite often because of his impatience with her. He seems to have regarded her as an irritant. It is all the more remarkable that Christine was able to maintain a tolerable relationship among the members of the family group, which, it must be remembered, included her illegitimate son Karl, whom Hebbel had adopted but whom he nonetheless resented. And it is most remarkable that her kindness and tact completely won over Elise. When she went back to Hamburg, it was Christine who kept up the correspondence. Elise's letters, written after her return to Hamburg, are full of gratitude for Christine's goodness. She no longer dared to even send Hebbel birthday greetings herself, but asked Christine to deliver the message because she knew that he attached no importance to what she might have to write. Hebbel continued, however, to contribute to Elise's support and to the support of Christine's son, Karl Hebbel, whom Elise took back with her to Hamburg and reared as her own child.

Thus, at least to some degree reconciled with her lot, Elise lived out the few remaining years of her life, lavishing upon the boy Karl and his half-sister Tine Hebbel the love that had been the due of her own children. Occasionally the Hebbels would come to Hamburg on business or for a guest performance of Christine. These reunions were a mixture of pain and happiness for Elise, for Hebbel was frequently cruel to her. In a letter to him dated April 10, 1853, she wrote: "You will never get rid of your violent temper, at least not as concerns people with whom you do not dissemble. You wrote me once yourself, 'If I were to cease losing my temper, I would have to become hypocritical.' Only your outbreaks of temper since I was in Vienna and now these two times here were always mixed with a hateful bitterness toward me, and you always tried to belittle me."[6] The hateful bitterness of which Elise complains reminds one of the hateful bitterness, much more violent and relentless, to be sure, with which Hebbel wrote of Kirchspielvogt Mohr after he had persuaded himself that Mohr had stifled his mental growth. Christine, however, continued to be the one person who linked Elise with life and love. In a letter of February, 1850, the latter wrote to her: "That our relationship to one another turned out to be so pure I owe to being there, to your urging me to come to Vienna. No matter how many hours of grief awaited me there in that unforgettable city, never would it all have come out this way if I had not gotten to know you and everything there personally. Now our relationship is certainly one of the most unusual that can be."[7]

Elise's health, never robust, became ever more frail. Some weeks after her death, Hebbel wrote in his diary, in a brief review of the year just past: "Elise is no more. She departed from this life towards morning on the eighteenth of December, 1854. There had been no hope for her for a long time before, and death was therefore to be wished for. For this reason the sad news did not shake me at the moment it arrived so much as it quivered within me afterwards and will continue to do so. What a disordered life, how deeply intertwined with my own and still contrary to the will of nature, and without the right spiritual relationship! Nonetheless, there is no one I will be more ready to encounter in the fairer regions, when they are opened to me hereafter."

CHAPTER 6

Two Failures and a Triumph

HEBBEL did not long retain his role as literary lion of Vienna, and for a while he and his wife led a rather lonely life. He did, however, have the satisfaction that *Maria Magdalene* received an effective performance in Leipzig, followed by other performances elsewhere. As a result, he became the subject of a certain amount of literary debate.

In the fall of 1846, Hebbel began work on a new play, *Ein Trauerspiel in Sizilien*, which, despite its title, he thought of not as a tragedy, but as a tragicomedy. This he describes in the dedication to Heinrich Theodor Rötscher, editor of the *Jahrbücher für dramatische Kunst*: "[Tragicomedy] is the result when a tragic destiny appears in an untragic form, where, on the one hand, the struggling and defeated individual is represented, and, on the other, not justified moral force, but a bog of foul conditions, which consumes thousands of victims without being worthy of a single one." Such conditions he believed he had seen in Italy. In this play he therefore had in mind to portray the terrifying aspect of the police state, the agents of which may be corruptible, and also the extremes of the problem of possession (diary entry of January 30, 1847).

The setting of the play is the entrance to a forest where the two gendarmes, Ambrosio and Bartolino, are on guard against robbers. Ambrosio is a braggart who is able to persuade the dull-witted Bartolino of the truth of almost any improbable tale. After both their imaginations become inflamed with thoughts of robbery and murder, they retire to do their devotions at the foot of a wayside statue of the Madonna and child. Angiolina appears. She is the daughter of Anselmo, who has had the misfortune of becoming hopelessly indebted to the wealthy Gregorio, the local *podestá*. Gregorio, an old man, wishes to marry the beautiful Angiolina, in order to enjoy the envy which his possession of her will elicit, and he threatens to ruin Anselmo if he does not permit the marriage. For this reason Anselmo has so vehemently rejected the suit of Angiolina's lover, Sebastiano, that Angiolina has come to a rendezvous in the forest in order to be married in secret to him. Since she has arrived before Sebastiano, Ambrosio and Bartolino are able to rob and murder her without interference. Thereupon they conceal themselves and wait for Sebastiano, whom Angiolina has told them she was expecting. When Sebastiano does arrive, the two villains arrest him on the pretended charge of murder. Then Gregorio and Anselmo enter the scene. After some questioning of Ambrosio and Bartolino, Gregorio begins to wonder whether they are not the murderers after all. This suspicion inspires a fruit thief, who had been hidden in a tree all the time and had seen what happened, to reveal the truth. Ambrosio takes the blame for everything upon himself, and Sebastiano promises to care for Angiolina's father, who, now that he no longer has a daughter to bestow, will be driven into poverty by Gregorio.

The play, of course, is an unintentional farce, but it was not so regarded by Hebbel, who, as we have seen before, took himself far too seriously to realize that his sense of humor was too bitterly grotesque to be acceptable. Instead, in the dedication to Rötscher which already has been cited, he wrote: "I hope that it will perhaps give you the opportunity to establish the theory of the category to which it belongs, and to enrich the science of esthetics with a new treatise. When it appeared for the first time some years ago in the *Novellenzeitung*, it was, presumably because of the title, almost everywhere taken to be a tragedy, although every verse, from the first to the last, contradicted this view in tone and coloration. And for this reason it received very odd reviews. This proves that there is something here for the esthetician to do."

Concurrently with his work on *Ein Trauerspiel in Sizilien*, Hebbel was composing another play of social criticism, the third of the group which includes *Maria Magdalene* and the tragicomedy just described. The name of this play was *Julia*, and it was not completed until October 23, 1847, although it had been begun nearly two years earlier, in November, 1845. Parenthetically, it may be said that working on two different plays at the same time was not unusual with Hebbel. For example, he began work on *Herodes und Mariamne* on February 23, 1847, before the completion of either *Julia* or *Ein Trauerspiel in Sizilien.*

In *Julia* Hebbel repeated the basic situation of *Maria Magdalene,* but whereas he understood the problem and the characters of the latter play from within, he had no such insight into the problems he was dealing with in *Julia.* The plural "problems" is used here advisedly, for the social criticism of *Julia* is directed not only at the overly rigid middle-class morality which we saw in *Maria Magdalene,* but also against two other ills of contemporary society, brigandage and decadence, which Hebbel had learned about in Italy. The result is an especially frosty and lifeless drama.

The setting of *Julia* is the Italy of Hebbel's time, and the central figure is an Italian Klara, named Julia, whose father, Tobaldi, is an exaggerated Meister Anton, more extreme and less aware of his relation to the Absolute than his German counterpart. Julia herself, however, is not an exact parallel to Klara, because she loves the father of her unborn child and has left her father's house in order to find her lover or learn why he never returned to claim her as he had vowed he would. When Tobaldi discovers that Julia has left his home, he spreads the false report that she is ill of a dangerous disease, and when she does not return, he proceeds to arrange a mock funeral for her. Meanwhile Julia, convinced that her lover, Antonio, has abandoned her, has hired a guide to take her through a forest in the hope that he will murder her for the money he knows she has upon her person. She is saved, however, by the intervention of a wealthy German count named Bertram, who has led a life of such physical and moral excesses that he is little more than a walking corpse, but with noble sentiments.

When Bertram learns Julia's story, he persuades her to let him play the part of her seducer and enter into a merely formal marriage with her in order to save the unborn child. He feels that by saving the life of Julia and of the child he will somehow make up for the life he has thrown away, and he exacts from her the promise that, if she should meet Antonio in the future, she will tell Bertram what her feelings are: if she still loves Antonio, Bertram will disappear from her life. After an unsuccessful effort to win over Tobaldi, Count Bertram takes Julia to one of his estates in the Tyrol. They are followed thither by Antonio, who has spied upon the funeral and suspects something unusual.

In his interview with Julia Antonio explains that he is the son of Grimaldi, the man whom Tobaldi drove into outlawry. He, Antonio, was, by force of circumstance, born outside the pale of society, and thus compelled to become a brigand. His whole life purpose had been to take vengeance on Tobaldi. He had planned to achieve his goal by despoiling Julia, but his feelings for her turned to love, and he had truly intended to take her with him as his wife. But then he had suffered a serious wound, which kept him bed-ridden for weeks, and he had no one whom he could trust to take a message to Julia. When Bertram comes upon him and Julia, he soon understands that Julia is still inwardly true to her love. There ensues a contest in generosity and nobility of soul. Antonio is so impressed by Bertram's readiness to take his own life in order to remove the obstacle to Antonio's union with Julia that he is willing to go back to Italy without her. She, in turn, does not wish to owe her happiness to the suicide of a man who has so magnanimously saved her life. Moreover, Antonio vows that he will watch over Bertram so that suicide will be impossible. Bertram, however, in an aside, expresses his intention to have an accident while hunting chamois in the mountains. And thus the play comes to a close that can almost be called a happy ending. If it is not a happy ending, it is not because Bertram has resolved to kill himself, for his life is already used up and death will be only the formal termination. It is rather because the play, as is usual with Hebbel, has a meaning beyond itself. That is, a certain form of society, the form that we have already seen in *Maria Magdalene,* has become so hardened and fixed that the individuals constituting that society have no room to move and breathe. This is, at least theoretically, as true for Tobaldi as for Meister Anton, and, of course, for the victims of the society. But to what rival form of society can the victims look to replace the old one? The only successful opposition comes from the libertinism of Bertram, but its success is obtained only at the expense of making propagation of the individual impossible. Decadence does not promise a much brighter future than does ruthless convention.

It was during his work on the two Italian plays and the first part of *Herodes und Mariamne* that Hebbel's third son, Emil, was born and died, followed, a little later, by his second son, Ernst. As we know, soon thereafter Elise came to Vienna and lived with the Hebbels for about a year. On Christmas Day, 1847, a daughter, Christine (Titi), was born. And so the year which had begun so inauspiciously came to a relatively calm and happy close.

In the world at large, however, these were days of great unrest. The Paris revolution of February 22, 1848, set off a series of revolutionary actions, not the least important of which took place in the Austrian Empire, especially in Vienna, where street-fighting broke out late in May and barricades were erected. Thereupon, the Emperor Ferdinand and his court moved to Innsbruck, to the great dismay and alarm of the Viennese, who felt that his presence would help to insure stability during the emergence of constitutional government. Many petitions were sent to Innsbruck begging the Emperor to return to Vienna, among them one sent by the Concordia literary association. The deputation of the Concordia consisted of four members, one of them Hebbel. After some delay, it was granted an audience with the Emperor and also with Archduke Franz Karl. To the latter, according to Emil Kuh,[1] Hebbel spoke up manfully: "Imperial Highness! There is ample mistrust, not of the Emperor's house, but of the surroundings of the imperial house, of persons, some of whom are present at this very moment in your antechamber! Against these persons all the arrows of the people are directed. In order to protect themselves, they array themselves before the Emperor and assert that they are protecting him; indeed, they say that the arrows are directed against him!" At this the Archduke is said to have blushed and replied, "I understand."

Despite the rioting in the streets and his strong interest in the events of the day, Hebbel completed the play that may well be considered his masterpiece on November 14, 1848. It surely marks the point where Hebbel turned definitely from realistic to poetic drama. Its title is *Herodes und Mariamne,* and it is based upon the *Jewish Antiquities* and *History of the Jewish Wars* by Flavius Josephus (A.D. 37-100). The main characters are Herod the Great, King of Judea at the birth of Christ;

[91]

his queen, Mariamne; his mother-in-law, Alexandra; his sister Salome; his brother-in-law, Joseph; his trusted friend, Soemus; and Sameas, the Pharisee.

The situation of Herod at the beginning of the play is, indeed, as he says, like that of the man in the fable who stands on a nest of serpents while attacked from in front by a lion, from behind by a tiger, and from above by a vulture. Herod's claim to legitimacy as King of the Jews stemmed from his being married to Mariamne, the last in the line of the Maccabees. But he drew not only his political strength from her but also his strength as a human being, for he prized her no less than his crown. Mariamne's mother, Alexandra, however, hates her son-in-law with an implacable passion intensified by her lust for power, and has leagued herself with Sameas the Pharisee, who tries to incite the populace to revolt on religious grounds. She has succeeded in having her son, Aristobulus, a frivolous youth of eighteen, elevated to the office of High Priest, which is the equal and the potential rival of the kingship, her purpose being, of course, to use Aristobulus to further her ambitions.

Realizing the danger to himself, Herod has the young man drowned in circumstances that are camouflaged to look accidental. Mariamne is, of course, shocked by the death of her brother and by the ruthless action of her husband; and Herod fears a long-lasting or even permanent estrangement, for he has revealed to her aspects of his character that might very well kill her love for him. Mariamne, however, who has a good deal of the strength and resolution of her ancestors, can understand the necessity for Herod's action and, once over the shock, would have forgiven the deed, had Herod not put on mourning in order to force acceptance of the pretense of accidental drowning. Alexandra, who now has the added incentive of avenging her son's death, has established communication with Antonius, the Roman overlord, at whose pleasure Herod wears his crown. She has written to Antonius, accusing Herod of murdering Aristobulus, and has sent, besides, a portrait of the extraordinarily handsome youth. She has also let it be known to Antonius, a notorious lecher, that Mariamne resembles her late brother but far exceeds him in beauty—a broad hint that the death of Herod would leave Mariamne a desirable widow. Herod has also sent Antonius a written account of the death of Aristobulus, but Antonius has refused to read it, and has summoned Herod before him to face possible execution for the death of the youth.

Before Herod leaves in obedience to the summons, Mariamne comes to him on the pretext of asking him to cease sending her gifts of magnificent pearls, if he does not want his sister, Salome, who hates Mariamne bitterly, to kill her out of envy. As their conversation unfolds, Herod tries to demonstrate the necessity of his action and goes on to say that their present leave-taking might very well be their last, since he has been summoned before Antonius. Now he asks her whether he should try to defend himself or not, for without her love, life would be worthless to him; and he finally asks her to take an oath to kill herself if Antonius should have him executed, for he cannot bear the thought of her surviving him for someone else to make his own.

Mariamne refuses, although, as she says to herself, she would surely feel such grief at his death that of her own accord she would plunge the dagger into her heart. Her motive in refusing is that she must restore the confidence and trust that once, as she thought, bound them to each other. If she took such an oath, she asks, what would guarantee that she would keep it? Only herself, her character. Therefore, since an oath is ultimately based on hope and trust, she urges him to see that he must dispense with the oath, for it is worse than meaningless, leading only to further estrangement. Alone, Herod, tormented by the thought of Mariamne in Antonius' arms, resolves to find someone who will kill her if he fails to return. As if in answer to his need, Salome's husband, Joseph, comes to bid him farewell, and he persuades Joseph that he will not be safe from Alexandra and Mariamne, once he, Herod, is dead, because he was involved in the drowning of Aristobulus. Out of fear Joseph undertakes to carry out Herod's commands.

During Herod's absence, Alexandra urges Sameas, the Pharisee, to incite the populace to riot in order to make it seem to Antonius that Herod's government is so poor that the rule of law has been impaired. Therefore, so Alexandra reasons, Antonius will not hesitate to have Herod killed in order to make Mariamne accessible. Alexandra also continues her attempts to make Mariamne hate Herod, but Mariamne does not care about new evidence that Herod is guilty of Aristobulus' death and puts the actual blame upon her mother, in whose presence she then freely takes the oath which Herod had asked for, namely to kill herself if he dies. By this time, Herod has been so long away that Joseph is very nearly convinced that he will never return. He withdraws the Roman guard from the Queen and her mother, and substitutes a Galilean, who will be faithful to him, come what may. His conversation with Mariamne and Alexandra convinces him that he must have them killed or be killed himself. Alexandra senses the danger and points it out to Mariamne, who wrings his terrible secret from him by trapping him in contradictions and half-admissions. The discovery of what Herod has done makes her see all her previous life as a dream: only now does she face the reality of life.

Herod, however, has not been put to death, but comes home unexpectedly to find that Mariamne knows of the orders he had given Joseph, and inflamed by Salome's senseless jealousy of Mariamne, the terrible suspicion rises in him that there is only one way in which she could have learned the secret, namely through being intimate with Joseph. Without giving Joseph a chance to speak, he has him executed. Now more than ever Mariamne refuses even to discuss the questions which torment Herod, because to do so would demean her. At this point a messenger from Antonius arrives, summoning Herod to come to his aid in the struggle against Octavian by preventing the rebellious Arabs from throwing their forces into the imminent battle. For Herod, who feels sure that Antonius will lose the struggle, this summons is tantamount to death, but to Mariamne it means that the wheel of time has been turned back, and that the situation is now as it was before Herod left for Alexandria: if he acts differently this time, if he shows that his order to Joseph was not symptomatic of his character, but was an aberration, then she will forget what has happened, as though he had struck her in delirium. Herod, however, feels that, having gone as far as he did, he must go farther, from fear that she will hold a wedding feast upon his grave as a kind of revenge. He therefore repeats his orders, this time naming his trusted friend, Soemus, regent during his absence.

Soemus, however, is a very different man from the slow-witted and timid Joseph. Whereas Joseph was unable to keep the secret, Soemus is determined to reveal it to Mariamne because he feels that Herod has desecrated humanity in thus dealing with them as mere vehicles of his pleasure. It is immediately plain to him that Herod's order is a sentence of death passed upon himself as well as Mariamne, for if he carries it out, the populace will avenge the death of Mariamne upon him and, if Herod returns safe, he will have to perish for his knowledge of Herod's secret.

The effect of Soemus' revelation upon Mariamne is devastating. Her first impulse is to kill herself, but she thinks better of it because this deed is what Herod had tried to exact from her. She therefore proclaims a great festivity to make it appear that she rejoices at being still alive. In the midst of the dancing Herod returns unheralded, to be informed that his presumed death was being celebrated. He orders Soemus' execution and a trial for Mariamne on a charge which he cannot clearly formulate. The intimidated judges pass the sentence of death upon her. Just before her execution, she tells the Roman captain, Titus, what she has refused to tell Herod, exacting from him the promise to keep silent until after she is dead. Thus she brings about an ironical and tragic triumph over the force which has killed her. She whom Herod had degraded by making her the instrument of his pleasure, retaliates by making Herod the unwitting instrument of her voluntary death.

At the exact hour of Mariamne's death, three kings, arrayed in splendor and bearing gifts, arrive in Herod's palace to do homage to his house. When they learn that no son has been born to Herod but rather that his wife has just died, they ask whether there is another royal line in the land. Upon receiving the information that there are still some descendants of David in Bethlehem, the kings go on, promising that, if they find the child they seek, they will return to Herod to tell him so that he can venerate the child also. Immediately after their departure, Titus comes to announce the death of Mariamne and to reveal her innocence to Herod, who is brought to full realization of what he has done only when Alexandra tells him that Mariamne had, of her own accord, sworn not to survive him. Now, bereft of everything else in the world that gave value to his life, Herod has only his crown, and this he is determined to hold against all odds. But the odds are overwhelming: even though, in order to exterminate the line of David from which the three kings had prophesied that the Supreme King would arise, he commands the slaughter of children who have been born within the year, the new era of Christianity cannot be held back.

The scene of the three kings, which was completely misunderstood in the first performance, is intended to indicate the perspective from which the events of the play should be viewed. Once again Hebbel was concerned with representing the metaphysical dualism, the conflict between the Whole and the part. Herod represents a form of the Idea in which the individual is of no account, whereas Mariamne and Soemus stand for the sanctity of the individual. They are crushed by Herod but they go down defiant, a sign that the form of the Idea which they represent will emerge once more. That it will not merely re-emerge but will be victorious, is guaranteed by the birth of Christ, who will usher in a new epoch.

Fortunately, the play is impressive and even overwhelming without reference to Hebbel's metaphysics. In this play he has mastered the use of blank verse, even though he does not use it with the suppleness he exhibits in the later *Gyges und sein Ring*. But here he has made it into an instrument he can play with a certain virtuosity: Herod's speeches, in which he pleads for the assurance of Mariamne's love and tells of his overwhelming passion for her, are eloquent and convincing, contributing greatly to the effectiveness of the characterization.

But the characterization depends also upon the remarkably subtle as well as complicated interplay of personality. As an example we can take the scene in the second act, where Mariamne wrings the secret from Joseph. Joseph, as we know, has undertaken to kill Mariamne in case of Herod's death because Herod has persuaded him that she will take vengeance upon him for his part in the death of Aristobulus. In Herod's protracted absence, Joseph becomes increasingly nervous and takes measures which Mariamne interprets as threatening her life. When Joseph is unable to swear that he intends her no harm, she shakes his composure by telling him that she has vowed to take her own life in the event of Herod's death, a vow, which, had Joseph known of it, would have made it unnecessary for him to plan to kill her. Then she dares him to kill her on the spot, and when he has not the courage to do so, she threatens to find some way to appeal to the Roman captain,

Titus, so that she can take revenge on him exactly as Herod would, could he know of Joseph's plan to kill her. Joseph fatuously seizes upon this formulation and says that he will hold her to her word to punish him exactly as Herod would. When Joseph repeats that he will hold her to her word, terrible suspicions begin to rise in Mariamne's heart, and she says that his words make it seem as though Herod himself had appointed her as the sacrificial victim and Joseph as the sacrificial priest. Joseph says that if this should be the case, Mariamne need not see anything so dreadful in it, indeed, it would be no more than proof that Herod loved her more than ever man loved woman. These words have the ring of familiarity, for they are reminiscent of what Herod said to Mariamne when pleading for her to vow to take her life if he were killed. Joseph continues: "Ich dächte doch, es könnte dir nur schmeicheln, / Wenn ihm der Tod nicht halb so bitter wär', / Als der Gedanke, Dich...." (I should think it could only flatter you if death were not half so bitter to him as the thought...). Mariamne interrupts: "Was gilt die Wette, / Ich selber bring' es jetzt für dich zu Ende! / Als der Gedanke, mich zurückzulassen / In einer Welt, wo ein Antonius lebt!" (What will you wager that I cannot complete your sentence for you? "Not half so bitter as the thought of leaving you behind in a world in which Antonius lives."). With that she has attained the terrible certainty.

Skill in verse and subtlety of characterization are not the only things that contribute to the greatness of this play. Its impressiveness comes also from its remarkable structure. The first scene exhibits a combination of analytic and synthetic exposition which quickly and compellingly sets the stage and presents Herod to us in a welter of venomous domestic hatred, maintained in his position against the fanaticism of the Pharisees by Rome, whose vassal he is. The action rises rapidly and forcefully to the climax at the end of the third act, where Herod, commanded by Antonius to prevent the Arabs from joining forces with Octavian, resolves to give Soemus the same instructions he had given to Joseph. Then comes the fourth act, often the act in which interest is likely to flag. Not so here. Soemus, a bold and resolute man, compels the Queen, who has been avoiding him, to admit him to her presence so that he may betray to her the secret, for he feels that Herod has reduced him no less than her to the status of a thing. This is followed by the great festivity with its magnificent setting and the bustle of preparation. Then the dance itself, observed by the uncomprehending Alexandra, Salome, and Titus. Mariamne joins in the dancing, disappears, and returns to the foreground. As she makes a sudden turn, she catches sight of herself in a mirror, just as she had once seen herself in a dream. In the dream there had been a mirror, just like the real one, in which she saw her entire life. First she appeared to herself as a child, then came the image of the maiden wooed by Herod; after that the dream grew uncanny and showed her herself in situations still to come, among them the present one, in the midst of the festivity. Then the light became ashen, and she herself, pale and bloodless. At this point, a shudder seized her in the dream and she cried out: "Jetzt komme / Ich als Geripp, und das will ich nicht seh'n" (Now I will appear as a skeleton, and that I do not want to see). At that instant, voices are heard in the background, "The King!" Herod strides in to be met by Mariamne crying out: "Der Tod! Der Tod! Der Tod ist unter uns! / Unangemeldet, wie er immer kommt!" (It's death, it's death, it's death among us! Unheralded as he always comes!). After this second climax, more powerful than the first, the rest of the action, as it has been outlined, follows rapidly.

CHAPTER 7

Lesser Pieces and a Fragment

THE year 1849 saw Hebbel occupied with various concerns. He had given up active interest in politics after being decisively beaten in his candidacy for the post of representative in the Frankfurt Parliament, but he continued to observe political developments with growing conservatism and intensified German nationalism. Apropos of the dispute between Denmark and Prussia over Schleswig and Holstein, he expressed his opinion that there was only one solution for Denmark, namely to become a German province. In fairness to Hebbel, however, it must be added that this bit of chauvinistic ingratitude is somewhat offset by his sense of sadness at the death of Christian VIII some two years before. Despite his arrogant attitude toward the Danes and the conservative drift of his orientation to politics, he deplored the renewed tide of reaction as much as the revolutionary spirit which had preceded it.

His literary activities were rather varied. In May, 1848, *Maria Magdalene* had been performed for the first time in Vienna, a direct result of political liberalization, which afforded him only little pleasure: "The Hofburgtheater is going to perform my plays," he wrote in his diary on March 28, 1848, "Holbein [the director] informed me of it personally this morning. If only I were childish enough to be able to be happy about it. I don't like the taste of the egg that has been roasted in the world conflagration." Like it or not, Hebbel in this way had his plays performed, at least as long as Holbein was the director. On February 14, 1849, Christine appeared in a successful production of *Judith,* but the first performance of *Herodes und Mariamne* on April 18 was totally misunderstood, the scene of the three kings actually provoking mirth. Later in the year, on November 21, a new play, *Der Rubin,* which Hebbel had composed between April 1 and May 19, was unsuccessfully performed.

Der Rubin, subtitled *A Fairy-Tale Comedy in Three Acts,* is set in ancient Baghdad and is the story of a very poor and honest young fisherman named Assad, who, upon being shown a tray of jewels, both false and genuine, suddenly conceives a passion for a ruby of surpassing beauty. When the owner quite naturally refuses to give him the gem, Assad simply takes it, but he is caught by the Kadi, that is, the judge who metes out punishment for transgressions against religious law. Assad refuses to give up the ruby, preferring to die rather than let it out of his hands. As he is about to be executed for the theft, an old man named Irad, a wizard, rescues him by making him invisible and carrying him off to another part of Baghdad. Here he explains to Assad that the Caliph's beautiful daughter, Fatime, has been imprisoned in the ruby by a wicked sorcerer who has set certain extremely difficult conditions for her rescue. But Assad can temporarily release Fatime from her sleep by kissing the ruby three times at midnight. Assad does so and is, of course, overwhelmed by her beauty. He learns from her that what he must do to rescue her is something so simple that he can readily do it, but is at the same time an impossibility for him.

Having imparted this information, the princess returns to her magic prison. The following day, Assad is once again caught by the Kadi's men. On this day, the Caliph, who still mourns the loss of his daughter so intensely that he plans to leave his throne in order to become a desert dervish, has decreed that he will preside at criminal trials. Therefore Assad, accused of robbery and violence, is brought before him. The Caliph gently asks Assad for the stone. Assad holds it out but then refuses to hand it to the Caliph. When the Caliph orders the Kadi to strike Assad down, Assad hurls the ruby into the nearby river rather than allow it to come into anyone's hands but his own. As he is about to stab himself, Fatime's voice is heard in the distance, and in a few moments she herself appears and is reunited with her father and with Assad, who, by throwing away the stone, has fulfilled the condition of her release. The Caliph bestows his daughter upon Assad and abdicates in favor of his new son-in-law. Assad, instructed by the wizard, Irad, that he can successfully rule over his millions of subjects if he does not forget that he himself is only one of them, begins his reign by decreeing a general amnesty so that the blessings of those pardoned will give him strength, courage, and wisdom to reign well. He asks Irad to remain at his side as his counselor, but Irad replies that the period of his might has come to an end, and that the wicked sorcerer's time is now at hand. It is, therefore, not entirely certain that Assad will be able to carry out his good intentions as he would like to.

This play, which is a dramatization of a fairy-tale written in 1837 and published in 1843 in the journal *Freihafen*, edited by Theodor Mundt, seems, at first, to be wholly uncharacteristic of Hebbel. Actually, however, it is closely related to his work and thought. In a diary entry of October or November, 1836, he had written, "Throw away in order not to lose—that is the best maxim." *Der Rubin* is, in a sense, an extended commentary on the maxim, and has a hidden connection with the predicament of Herod, for whom it was simply impossible to see that in order to retain what he most cherished, he had to be ready to let it go. Another connection with *Herodes und Mariamne* lies in the portrayal of oriental despotism. The Kadi and the Caliph dispose of human life and happiness with utmost indifference to the feelings of the individual. On one occasion, the Caliph, who at that time deemed himself a kind of innovator, broke the law of the Koran in regard to wine, and in his drunkenness killed one of his wives, Fatime's mother. For this reason the Caliph is not as insensitive to the welfare of his subjects as are his underlings, but he nonetheless is the representative of a form of the Idea which bears the seeds of its own destruction within itself, just as does Herod's despotism. Assad, as the representative of a new form, will not forget that he is only a poor fisherman's son. Whether or not Assad will be entirely successful, is, as has been noted, put in some doubt by the circumstance that Irad, the good wizard, must, in his turn, relinquish power to the wicked sorcerer. If Allah has intervened in Assad's life and made everything work for the best, from now on Assad must rely upon his merely human endowments.

Hebbel himself wrote and published a review of the unsuccessful performance in the *Österreichische Reichszeitung*, of which he was for a brief time a contributing editor. Here he wrote quite openly that the play had failed in spite of all that the director, Franz von Holbein, the actors, and the musicians did to save it. The reason for the failure, he went on, lay entirely within the play itself and in its relationship to the conceptions which the theater-going public had of fairy-tale and comedy writing. Having made this handsome and justified admission, Hebbel went on to point out that such acknowledged masterpieces of comedy as Heinrich von Kleist's *Der zerbrochene Krug* and Franz Grillparzer's *Weh dem, der lügt,* had also failed in their first performances. This comparison, of course, did nothing to convince the critics, who found in the play neither clarity of conception nor poetic elevation, nor any touch of humor or flight of the imagination. It seems that comedy was really not Hebbel's métier.

The hostility of almost all the Viennese critics might have weighed more heavily on Hebbel had it not been for a circle of ardent admirers, chief of whom was Emil Kuh, who later became Hebbel's principal biographer. Almost everyone who met Hebbel felt the force of his personality and intellect. Many were repelled, but just as many were fascinated by his seemingly demonic power. Some, young men of a rather soft and gentle nature, fell wholly under his spell and, for a while at least, seemed to live only through him.[1] Among the members of Hebbel's circle at this time were, in addition to Emil Kuh, such personalities as Julius Glaser, who later became Minister of Justice in Austria; Karl Werner, later a teacher of literature and school official; Karl Debrois van Bruyck, a musical and literary talent; the painter Karl Rahl, who has left us a portrait of Hebbel; and various other young men who were interested in the arts. Their meetings with Hebbel were likely to be rather solemn and rapt. The conversation was more of a monologue, which began soon after Hebbel had, with an expansive gesture, asked them to be seated.

To an unsympathetic observer, such as the novelist Alfred Meissner, it seemed as though, as soon as the seance began, one could read a feeling of their own insignificance in the faces of the disciples as they waited for the master to speak. On the occasion which Meissner describes,[2] the conversation soon turned to Hegel, and the merits and deficiencies of his esthetics were discussed. Then Hebbel began to speak about his *Judith.* His solemnity increased. With the sacred fire of a priest proclaiming how his god was revealed to him, he described how

Judith and Holofernes had first risen before his imagination.

A less hostile writer, Eduard Hanslick, known for his opposition to the music of Richard Wagner, confirms Meissner's description of the one-sidedness of a conversation with Hebbel,[3] whom he calls a virtuoso of elocution who reveled in his virtuosity. "I have rarely heard anyone say such original and profound things and discourse with such perfection of form, such readiness for the printer. He never had to change a word, not a single mark of punctuation was omitted. Listening to Hebbel was a rare pleasure. In this pleasure I found only one peculiarity of Hebbel disturbing. As he spoke, he came closer and closer to the person he was addressing, so that his breath struck the latter. I usually retreated imperceptibly until my back was to the wall and I could go no farther. In all this, Hebbel had the habit of rocking his head rhythmically to the right and to the left, while gesturing with his right hand."

As long as the hostile critics merely criticized his work, Hebbel was delighted to accept the challenge and enter into debate with them. But when Heinrich Laube became artistic director of the Hofburgtheater, he found his position very difficult. Laube, belonging to the persuasion known as Young German, which saw the purpose and justification of literature in the attempt to bring about certain political and social reforms and to champion liberal ideas, could scarcely be expected to appreciate Hebbel's attempts to present symbolic pictures of universal human and philosophical import. And Hebbel, of course, had a very low opinion of Laube's talents as a dramatist and an even lower opinion of him as a thinker. The result was not only that Hebbel's plays were not included in the repertoire, but also that Hebbel's wife was assigned to less important roles than those which she had been playing. As a consequence, the Hebbels had to arrange for Christine to give guest performances in theaters away from Vienna during her vacations. At the same time, Hebbel tried to interest various theater directors in his plays, attempts which eventually brought rich rewards.

Meanwhile he in no wise modified the principles which guided him in his dramatic composition. In June, 1849, he again took up a theme which had occupied his attention from time to time since January, 1837. By October, 1850, he had completed the second act, but he never got beyond that point except for some fragments and sketches. In many respects, the skeleton which we have of this play exhibits some of Hebbel's worst faults and is actually a bit ludicrous, but it is grandiosely conceived and surely significant for a study of Hebbel since he frequently expressed the hope that it would be his masterpiece. Masterpiece or not, it is called *Moloch,* and perhaps the fairest notion of Hebbel's intentions can be obtained from his own summary in a letter to Saint-René Taillandier of August 9, 1852.

"The drama," Hebbel writes, "will try to show that religious feeling *vis-à-vis* the highest powers is the root of the world. Hieram, a general in Hannibal's army, removes the Moloch idol from the flames of Carthage and takes it to Thule. However, he does so not because he still venerates the god, but only because he intends by means of the idol to win the allegiance of the barbarous people [i.e. the early Teutons]. When they have, in this way, attained some civilization, he intends to arm them against Rome. His plan succeeds insofar as it was moral; the people subject themselves to the god, and the fruits of this great religious act do not fail to appear: the foundations of the first institutions of civilization are laid, and state and church emerge in their rudimentary form. But at the same moment in which Hieram transgresses the boundary of what is moral—when he would like to make the god, which has bestowed light and benefaction, into a tool of his egotism—at that very moment he is destroyed by that god, by the belief of the people in him, a belief which Hieram has indeed sowed, but which he cannot kill. He dies in the conviction that the divine principle, even in its crudest form, is still more powerful than the most powerful man, and that the latter must yield. His work, however, survives him, insofar as it deserves to do so, and in the conclusion one looks into a world which becomes increasingly enlightened and transfigured with every day that passes."

Shortly after Hebbel completed the second act of *Moloch* he began work on a two-act play entitled *Michel Angelo,* which he finished, in less than two months, on December 18, 1850.

The short play is based on an anecdote from Michelangelo's biography to the effect that he buried one of his own statues where excavators were looking for relics of classical civilization.

The statue was found and was greatly admired as antique and superior to Michelangelo's own work. The great sculptor, however, was able to prove that it was his, and thus taught the envious critics a stinging lesson. This is essentially the plot of Hebbel's play, which ends with the moral pointed by both Michelangelo and Pope Julius. Michelangelo, having humiliated his detractors, asserts the duty of the gifted individual to trust in himself and pay his respects to his own genius, as well as to the genius of the more greatly gifted individual. Pope Julius acknowledges the justice of this view, but points out that the envious critics have a sort of satanic function: by their goading they drive the genius to greater exertion, until finally he has attained such heights that he can ignore them. In conclusion, the Pope brings Michelangelo around to a proper appreciation of the genius of Raphael. The application to Hebbel himself is readily understood.

This relatively mild way of dealing with hostile critics was not accorded Julian Schmidt in the essay "Abfertigung eines ästhetischen Kannegiessers" (Chastisement of an Esthetic Twaddle-Monger), published together with *Julia* in July, 1851. Schmidt had severely criticized Hebbel's work in an essay in the journal *Grenzboten*. The criticism enraged Hebbel, who demonstrated at length the absurdities and perfidies of Schmidt's criticism, which he felt questioned his integrity as a man and as a writer. In concluding his attack on Schmidt he wrote: "Germany has had, without a doubt, more significant creative writers than myself. But in one respect I am equal to the greatest of my predecessors: in the religious earnestness and the ethical strictness with which I practice my art I yield to no one. And even if I know nothing about my future, I know that my age cannot, *vis-à-vis* a later age, cast worse doubt upon its own moral beliefs than by means of the doubt which it casts upon my moral beliefs!"

CHAPTER 8

Schoolmaster to Royalty

IN the year 1851, Hebbel began to establish important connections with personalities outside of Vienna. Thus, on his trips to Berlin, where he arranged for guest-performances for Christine, he paid his respects to Ludwig Tieck, who considered him the most impressive man he had talked with since his encounter with Goethe. Others whom Hebbel got to know personally were Peter Cornelius, the painter, Karl August Varnhagen von Ense, and Theodor Mundt. But the most important personal connection was that with Franz Dingelstedt, who early in the year had become director of the Hoftheater in Munich. This was, strictly speaking, not a new acquaintance, for Hebbel had corresponded irregularly with Dingelstedt since 1840. But now the latter had chosen to present Hebbel's *Judith*, and the play had succeeded very well. Furthermore, Dingelstedt expressed interest in presenting more of Hebbel's plays, and soon the two men were exchanging cordial letters.

In view of the fact that Munich now had a special meaning for Hebbel, it is not surprising that his next play, *Agnes Bernauer*, deals with an episode in the history of Bavaria.

Agnes Bernauer was written in the extraordinarily short time between September 22 and December 17, 1851. Hebbel's interest in the material, however, went back to early 1845, when he conceived the idea of a tragedy of love and beauty with the following content: A marvelously beautiful and innocent girl leaves the convent where she has grown up. Her beauty arouses all sorts of passions in those who see her, mostly desire and envy. When the brother of the man she loves seeks to kill her lover, her horror at the terrible acts which she is unintentionally responsible for compels her to re-enter the convent. For such a theme, the story of Agnes Bernauer, who had to lose her life for the good of the state, was the perfect vehicle, and this, in turn, was affected and deepened by the experiences and insights Hebbel had gained from the political upheavals of 1848.

Agnes Bernauer is the most colorful of Hebbel's dramas, full of pageantry, with strongly contrasting scenes from late medieval Bavaria. It opens in the humble home of the barber-surgeon, Caspar Bernauer, whose daughter Agnes is known as the Angel of Augsburg. The term "angel" fittingly describes Agnes: hers is a perfect beauty of body and soul, and she is another Genoveva-figure, but not exalted to saintliness. Every man, whether young or old, who sees her, is drawn to her in love or desire. As a result, she has gained the enmity of all the young women of the city, although as they must admit in fairness, she has done nothing to take their sweethearts from them. Even Barbara, who has come to upbraid and reproach her, says that she should enter a convent in order to hide her fatal beauty. And Agnes, troubled that her former friends now hate and envy her, wonders whether she should not stay away from the tournament which is about to take place. Her father, however, readily persuades her that it makes no more sense for her to stay away than for the champion knight not to enter the tourney: on that principle the reward would go to the one who deserved it least.

And so she does go to the tournament. One of the participants is Duke Albrecht, son of the reigning Duke Ernst of München-Bayern. The two see each other at a distance, and at that moment their fate is sealed. Albrecht, unable to think of anything except the unknown beauty, orders his attendant nobles to find her. They have no success. But in the evening she comes with her father to the great ball that is to crown the day's festivities. After only a few words with her, Albrecht declares his love and asks Bernauer for her hand in marriage, totally disregarding the objections of the nobles, who have pointed out some of the practical consequences of his rashness. Caspar Bernauer also reminds him that only fifty years ago the occupation of barber-surgeon was dishonorable, and that his daughter could not have appeared at a tournament without being flogged for her presumption. Albrecht replies with reckless self-confidence: "And fifty years hence every angel who resembles her shall find a throne on earth, even if she owed her life to a man who has to kiss your hand. This shall be the effect of my example."

The following morning, the nobles, discussing the situation, are thoroughly alarmed by Albrecht's impetuosity, for the political situation of Bavaria is very precarious. Bavaria was not at that time a single duchy but was divided into three parts: Ingolstadt-Bayern, Landshut-Bayern, and München-Bayern, the latter being ruled jointly by the two Dukes, Ernst and his brother Wilhelm. Ernst's son Albrecht is the heir to the throne, but Wilhelm also has a son, the frail boy Adolph, who is next in line. But the rival dukes of Ingolstadt and Landshut are eager to annex as much territory as possible and would, of course, welcome any flaw in the succession that would give them the pretext for intervening. One of Albrecht's followers, Count Törring, undertakes to have a chat with Caspar Bernauer and persuades him that Albrecht is not really interested in marrying Agnes, but only in establishing a liaison that would guarantee her ease and security forever.

Albrecht arrives at this moment to find Bernauer glad that nothing will come of the perilous marriage proposal and assuring Count Törring that the Vehmic League would have the power to protect Agnes from further molestation by the Duke, while Agnes protests that she has sufficiently regained the use of speech to permit her to reply in her own name. To Albrecht she says, "God has made me, too, and He can make me greater if it is His holy will, or you lesser, for everything is on earth by way of trial, and lofty and lowly will have to exchange places sometime, if they do not meet His test. My lord, do not do anyone else such an injury as you have done me: one doesn't expect it of you and for that reason it is doubly bitter." Turning to her father, she asks him to place her in a convent, for she has lost everything except the dreadful memory of what has happened. Albrecht, however, repeats his proposal of marriage, and when Count Törring steps forward to say that he had acted on his own initiative and does homage to Agnes, all doubts in her heart are dispelled. Fully conscious of the inevitable grave consequences of their act, the barber-surgeon's daughter and the Duke are secretly married.

The third act opens in the workroom of Duke Ernst, who is shown meditating on the history and destiny of Bavaria, which it is his sole ambition to restore to some of its former greatness.

In his plans, Albrecht plays an important role, not only as the heir whose duty it will be to continue his father's work, but also by contracting a politically advantageous marriage. Ernst can, therefore, not believe his ears when Hans von Preising, his Chancellor, tells him that Albrecht is ignoring all messages and letters addressed to him, and has, instead, retired to his small castle of Vohburg with Agnes Bernauer. Duke Ernst is unable to grasp the full seriousness of the situation and rejects the idea that Albrecht and Agnes have secretly married, but directs Preising to summon Albrecht to a tournament at Regensburg. This tournament, he reasons, will clarify the situation, for he intends to announce Albrecht's betrothal to Princess Anna of Braunschweig, thus terminating an old and dangerous political rivalry.

Preising finds Duke Albrecht at Vohburg and informs him of Duke Ernst's plans for a marriage alliance with Braunschweig. Albrecht protests that he is unable to acquiesce: "Ich bin ein Mensch, ich soll dem Weibe, mit dem ich vor den Altar trete, so gut, wie ein And'rer, Liebe und Treue zuschwören, darum muss ich's so gut, wie ein And'rer, selbst wählen dürfen!" (I am a human being, and I must swear love and devotion to the woman with whom I go to the altar, just as well as anybody else, and therefore I must be allowed to choose her just as well as anyone). When Preising sees that he can accomplish nothing by further pleading, he summons Albrecht to the tournament and leaves. At the tournament, Duke Ernst publicly and formally seeks to bar Albrecht from participating, on the ground that the code governing such affairs forbids any nobleman guilty of seduction to tourney. Albrecht is, therefore, forced to reveal that Agnes is his wife and not his mistress. Ernst immediately proclaims his nephew Adolph his successor. Tumult breaks out. A spokesman for Duke Ludwig of Ingolstadt promises support to Albrecht. Ernst reminds everyone that he has the backing of the Emperor, calls for loyalty to his new heir, and cancels the tournament. Albrecht turns to the burghers and peasants for help.

Two and a half years later the young Duke Adolph sickens and dies. This was a probability Duke Ernst had reckoned with: immediately after the unfortunate tournament in Regensburg he had consulted the three greatest jurists of the day as to whether he had the right and duty to have Agnes put to death in order to avert great evil to the state. The three had agreed that such was indeed the case, merely because she had entered into marriage with Albrecht. The document which the judges had drawn up has been left unsigned, but now, with the death of Adolph, the time has come when it must be signed and executed. Preising finds it almost impossible to accept the necessity of putting to death this young woman whose only transgression it was, as he put it, that she did not take the veil. Ernst, who previously has been very skeptical of the purity of Agnes' motives, does not dispute Preising on this point. Instead, he asks him whether there can be any doubts or suspicions of the capacity or rectitude of the judges or of himself as Agnes' accuser. To this Preising must say no. Then Ernst points out that although the death sentence was passed two and a half years ago, it is still unsigned because he had left the decision to God: whether the sentence would be executed or not was to depend on whether or not Adolph lived, but God had taken the boy and thus given His answer. (Here, of course, we recognize another metaphysical experiment, like that made by Golo in *Genoveva*.)

Preising, although he recognizes that the succession to the throne cannot be disturbed without entailing civil war, still feels that there must be some solution. He has not, however, thought of one possibility that Ernst has entertained, that is, to name either Ludwig of Ingolstadt or Heinrich of Landshut as his successor; and when Ernst mentions it, he speedily rejects it as leading only to devastation of the country to which Ernst has brought prosperity. Preising then suggests having Agnes kidnapped and removed to some safe spot, but Ernst points out that this would lead to involuntary bigamy on Albrecht's part, a sin for which Ernst himself would be responsible. And finally Preising says that in extreme cases divorce has been resorted to, but Ernst asks how it will be possible to divorce Agnes from Albrecht when neither one wishes it. There remains, therefore, only the one possibility. Agnes must die, even though her death is sure to arouse Albrecht's fury and despair: Ernst makes another metaphysical experiment in signing the death warrant, for only God can decree the outcome, whether Albrecht will take his own life, or whether he will take to the field against Ernst. If the latter occurs the action will soon be over, for either Ernst will be quickly defeated or else the Emperor's troops will impose swift peace.

Preising makes one further effort to save Agnes' life. When Agnes has been imprisoned after being abducted in the absence of Duke Albrecht, he seeks her out and shows her that there is only one way for her to escape, and that is to denounce her marriage as sinful and enter a convent. The way out which is thus opened for her is a way she cannot take, for it would brand as iniquitous her holiest possession. Certain that Albrecht would sooner mourn her dead than feel himself betrayed by her and their love declared wrongdoing, she chooses to die and is hurled from a bridge into the Danube.

Ernst, at the head of his troops, awaits the outcome. What will Albrecht do when he learns what has happened? After some anxious waiting, he sees a distant village go up in smoke, a sign that rage has overcome despair in Albrecht's heart. In answer to Preising's question whether that which he wished to prevent is not now actually taking place, he confidently replies that the damage done on this one day can easily be undone, for the Emperor's forces will soon overwhelm Albrecht; and he speaks of a surprise.

For a time, Albrecht and Ludwig of Ingolstadt sweep everything before them, and Duke Ernst is taken prisoner. But no sooner does this happen than a change begins to take place in Albrecht, in whom feelings of respect and love for his father cannot be repressed. When an imperial herald and a papal legate read ban and excommunication over Albrecht, he begins to feel that he stands alone against the forces of law and religion, a feeling which is strengthened by Ernst's strong plea to think of his obligations to the future subjects whose happiness and welfare depend solely on him. The impression made by these words is strengthened when Ernst goes on to promise that full honors will be done Agnes as Albrecht's deceased Duchess; and Albrecht bows to his father as head of the state and representative of the Emperor. He is unable, however, to open his arms to embrace his father, who comes towards him with a gesture of perfect reconciliation. Thereupon Duke Ernst holds out his sceptre to Albrecht, saying: "Trag ihn ein Jahr in der Furcht des Herrn, wie ich! Kannst du mich dann nicht lossprechen, so ruf mich, und ich selbst will mich strafen, wie du's gebeutst! Im Kloster zu Andechs bin ich zu finden." (Bear it for one year in the fear of the Lord, as I have done. If then you cannot acquit me, summon me, and I will punish myself as you command! I can be found in the monastery at Andechs). His resistance now completely broken, Albrecht kneels, saying: "Vater, nicht vor Kaiser und Reich, aber vor dir!" (Father, not before Emperor and realm, but before you).

As the play stands, all the main characters undergo a tragic experience: Caspar Bernauer and Theobald, the apprentice, whose hopeless love cost him his life, as well as Albrecht, Agnes, and, most significant of all for Hebbel's view of tragedy, Duke Ernst himself. In the figure of Agnes, Hebbel develops one of his favorite themes, that the individual as such is in metaphysically guilty opposition to the Whole. Her only flaw was that she was beautiful and good, and for this—that is, for a flaw that is none by human standards—she had to die. In the character of Albrecht, however, although he is essentially good and in some ways admirable, one can readily find human flaws: his impetuosity, his recklessness, his failure to understand the nature of his, that is, the individual's, relationship to the Whole, until it is too late.

Hebbel intended the tragic predicament of Duke Ernst to be no less poignant, for as the perfectly justified representative of the universal forces he is compelled to require the death of someone of whose personal innocence he is convinced. More than this, he has found it necessary to perform two metaphysical experiments: he has disowned Albrecht as heir to the throne and named Adolph as his successor, and, upon the death of Adolph, he has risked his son's life by executing the death sentence pronounced on Agnes. He has resorted to these extreme measures in order to preserve the order for which he stands. Thus he has thrown away in order not to lose. And he does not lose, but the strain of what he has been through nearly breaks him. Just because he is the representative of the Idea, he is peculiarly exposed to tragedy as the instrument by means of which the Idea defends itself against the disruptive forces which Albrecht represents.

Whether or not Hebbel succeeded in grafting a political tragedy on to his originally conceived tragedy of love and

[112]

beauty is at least debatable. The beauty of Agnes, the dashing impetuosity of Albrecht, the unswerving fidelity of the lovers to each other, and their unhappy fate—all these things make a powerful appeal to the emotions of the audience and the reader, who may very well be unaffected by the reasons of state and the metaphysics of history. Hebbel's intention is plain enough, but it might be said with some justification that he has not fully realized it. And this may be because he had not, in his own mind, really fused the tragedy of love and beauty with that of statesmanship.

There are indications that Hebbel had differing conceptions of the role of Duke Ernst, and that he was unable to eliminate all traces of this. Thus it seems very odd to wait until the beginning of the third act to introduce the character who is the chief tragic figure of the play and the human antagonist of the lovers. It seems as though Ernst had been conceived as a much less important and sublime character. And then, at first, Ernst cannot believe that Agnes' relationship to Albrecht is anything but illegitimate; and at the tournament in Regensburg, when Albrecht has made it known that he is married to Agnes, Ernst feels only that Agnes must be a schemer who has seduced the young Duke for her selfish ends. Nonetheless, as we learn in the fourth act, Ernst makes no use of the death sentence passed upon her by the three worthiest judges of the time, but instead keeps the document in a sealed box and makes every effort to induce Albrecht to give up his claim to the succession. We receive no inkling of why Ernst has apparently had a change of heart and no longer regards Agnes as an upstart wench. Far from this; two and a half years later, when the populace is beginning to look upon Agnes as a witch because Duke Ernst's brother Wilhelm, Wilhelm's Duchess, and finally, their son, the boy Adolph, have all died since Agnes and Albrecht were married, Ernst can only agree with Preising that Agnes' sole transgression was that she did not shear her locks and take the veil. It does, therefore, seem at least possible that, in the course of working on the play, Hebbel's insight into the nature of the tragedy of statesmanship deepened, and that his point of view and his sympathies shifted so that Ernst emerged as the spokesman for Hebbel's conception of the exalted position of the state, as a stainless representative of the highest power who, merely by exhibiting the sublime conception of duty, subdues rebellious passion.

Shortly after the completion of *Agnes Bernauer,* Hebbel submitted his manuscript to Franz Dingelstedt to be considered for presentation in Munich. Since Dingelstedt's successful production of *Judith* in early April, 1851, the correspondence between director and playwright had been growing ever more cordial. Dingelstedt was greatly interested in the new play as sketched by Hebbel in his letters although he had some misgivings about producing it because the subject matter was all too familiar to Munich audiences. And then Melchior Meyr, a native Bavarian, submitted a dramatization of the same material before Hebbel had submitted his version. For a while there was some doubt whether it would be politic and advisable for Dingelstedt to reject Meyr's play in favor of one by a North German. Eventually, however, he concurred in the opinion, which Hebbel, whom he had allowed to read Meyr's manuscript, had of the play, that it was totally worthless; and preparations were made to stage Hebbel's play.

As part of these preparations, Dingelstedt invited Hebbel to come to Munich, an invitation which Hebbel gladly accepted. He arrived on February 22, 1852, and was soon in touch with the intellectual and social elite of the Bavarian capital. He was once again lionized, as he had been when the Zerbonis launched his career in Vienna; and once again he stood in the presence of a king as he had in Copenhagen, but this time he was there not as a humble petitioner but as an acknowledged literary genius. He went to the Royal Palace at the invitation of the scholar-king Maximilian II, who expressed his great enthusiasm for *Judith* and *Genoveva,* and a lively interest in the new play, *Agnes Bernauer.* Other members of the royal family requested the pleasure of Hebbel's company, including the lovely young Queen, and King Ludwig I, Maximilian's father, who had abdicated in favor of his son because of his involvement with the actress Maria (or Lola) Montez, who had taken an improper interest in affairs of state. When Hebbel outlined the plot of *Agnes Bernauer* to the King and explained the necessity of the girl's execution, the King, who had defended his favorite against her enemies, exclaimed that he would not have had the strength to act as did Duke Ernst. "And still," replied Hebbel, "Your Majesty would have been obliged to do so, had you been the ruler." The brick-layer's son had risen so far that he was now able to prescribe rules of conduct to royalty.

Unfortunately, the performance of *Agnes Bernauer* was not a success because improper political significance was attached to it. The confrontation of Albrecht and Ernst at the tournament, when Albrecht calls upon the populace to back him in his resolve to make Agnes his Duchess, was related to King Maximilian's more democratic and liberal principles as opposed to King Ludwig's autocratic rule. The fourth and fifth acts seemed thoroughly anticlimactical after the sensation caused by the misunderstood third act. The failure of the play had repercussions in Vienna, which greatly annoyed Hebbel, but he felt compensated later in the year by highly successful performances in Weimar and Stuttgart. Altogether, the year 1852 was a good one for Hebbel. Whatever difficulties it may have brought him, as he ended his diary he wished only that things might remain as they were.

CHAPTER 9

The Sleep of the World

THERE now ensued something of a pause in Hebbel's creativity, for he had undertaken to edit the works of Ernst von Feuchtersleben, a task which made greater demands upon his time than he had anticipated. He kept up a lively association with various notable members of the artistic and cultural elite. He corresponded with G. G. Gervinus, the literary historian, who treated literature against the background of political and cultural history, and also with Robert Schumann, who used *Genoveva* for an opera and set several of Hebbel's poems to music. It was not long, however, before Hebbel's creative powers were reawakened, this time by the remark of an acquaintance who was the librarian of the police headquarters of Vienna, Karl Braun von Braunthal. Braunthal called his attention to an article in *Pierers Universallexikon* about Herodotus' story of Gyges and Candaules.

Stimulated by the dramatic possibilities of this anecdote, Hebbel looked further into the matter and found that another version of the story was found in Plato's *Republic*. According to Herodotus, Candaules, King of Lydia, had a dear friend Gyges, also a Lydian, whom he wished to convince of his wife's peerless beauty. He arranged to have Gyges look upon her while she was naked. The Queen, nameless in Herodotus, becomes aware of the dishonor done to her and compels Gyges to kill either himself or Candaules. On the following night Gyges kills his friend Candaules, marries the Queen, and becomes King of Lydia. According to Plato, the son of Gyges, a herdsman in the service of the King, took from the finger of an unnaturally large body which he found in a cleft of the earth, a ring that made its wearer invisible. By means of the ring, he gained access to Candaules' Queen and won her favor. He married her after killing Candaules and thus became King.

Hebbel, in writing his play, combined various features of the two tales and made the nameless Queen, whom he called Rhodope, the central figure, depicting her as the representative of an ancient mixed Greek and Indian culture. In doing so, he drew heavily upon Georg Holzmann's adaptations of tales from India, *Indische Sagen,* which he had favorably reviewed. The first act of the play was finished on December 14, 1853. Work proceeded rather slowly, but on November 14, 1854, *Gyges und sein Ring* was completed.

Many critics consider this play to be Hebbel's best. It is surely his smoothest, most polished, and most "classical" drama. Hebbel himself felt that it was formally very close to the dramas of Racine, but in spirit far removed from them. He called its action prehistoric and mythical.

Kandaules, the last descendant of Heracles, has found his Queen in a land where the Greek and Indian cultures meet. Her father, the King, is the only man in whose presence she has appeared without her veil before her marriage to Kandaules. Far from resenting such restriction and trying to break out of the royal garden which was her world, and where she sat, rapt in dreams, beneath her plane tree, she did not wish to differentiate between herself and the All. Her existence scarcely constituted one pole of the tragic dualism which is the basic fact of the universe in Hebbel's view. Even when she left her home to take up her abode in Lydia as its Queen, she walled off the strange new world and continued her secluded existence almost as though she had never left her homeland, and as though her husband had, instead, left his.

Kandaules, to be sure, does not spend all his time in dalliance and contemplation in Rhodope's garden. He is far too active, too much of an individual, to accept her view of life or even to understand what it means to her. Although he was at first gratified that the only other man besides himself who had seen Rhodope without her veil was Rhodope's father, he did not understand or even wish to consider the possibility that the veil was part of her being. He needed the testimony of witnesses to her beauty in order to enjoy the sense of ownership, as the owner of precious stones must know that others envy him his possession of them if his satisfaction is to be complete. Rhodope, on the other hand, had grown up to accept entirely the terrible decree of her ancestral religion that a woman is dishonored, her chastity destroyed, if she is seen without her veil by anyone but her husband, and that the unchaste woman may not live.

The third of the principal characters is Gyges, a Greek, who has become the inseparable companion and friend of Kandaules ever since the day when they met on a tiger hunt. At that time, Kandaules, although aware that the animal was about to jump at him, allowed Gyges, in his youthful enthusiasm, to make the kill, letting him suppose that he was saving the King's life. Since that time, they have often hunted together and confided their inmost feelings to each other. Kandaules has spoken mostly of his Queen and her beauty, but Gyges, so innocent and inexperienced that he has not yet known the spell of woman, pays only scant attention. His indifference has been particularly galling to Kandaules, who, as we know, cannot feel assured that he has a jewel or a wife of unequaled beauty unless there are witnesses to confirm his good fortune.

When the play opens, Kandaules is getting ready to preside at the cultic games honoring Heracles, the founder of Lydia's ruling dynasty. His servant, Thoas, brings him the ancient gigantic sword and diadem, the legacy of Heracles, but Kandaules sharply demands the ones he has had made, a sword that can be wielded indoors and a diadem that fits an ordinary mortal's head. Thoas warns the King that the populace feels fear and reverence for the ancient things but none at all for the new. Kandaules nonetheless insists on carrying through his reform, for he, the rationalist, feels only scorn for mere tradition and demands of things that they be practical and useful. Gyges, who has been a witness to this scene, asks the King's permission to participate in the games.

Kandaules is very reluctant to grant the request because he feels that the Lydian contests require more brute strength of the participants than Gyges, the Greek, possesses. When, finally, Gyges succeeds in winning Kandaules' permission to compete, he presents him with a mysterious ring, which, when turned a certain way, has the power of disembodying its wearer, making him both invisible and impalpable. Gyges owes his life to this ring, which he found when taking refuge in a cave from robbers who were pursuing him, but he feels that only a king is

worthy of owning it. Kandaules, who is not awed by the supernatural powers of the ring, accepts it readily: he wishes to try
it out at once and does so. By means of the ring, he learns that
his people are dissatisfied with him for his peaceable nature and
rejection of traditional customs. Both vexed and amused by the
conversation he has overheard, he tells Rhodope of his magic
ring and what he has done with it. Her response, "How terrible," Kandaules takes to mean terrible for the wicked, who can
now easily be detected, but she urges him to hurl the ring into
the deepest river, for she feels that it is a thing that could destroy
the world. The King agrees to throw it away if Rhodope will
appear beside him, without her veil, at the games, a proposal
which she, of course, rejects as impossible.

At the games, Gyges wins all the prizes and also the enthusiastic admiration of the spectators, but at the ceremonial feast
which follows the contests, he falls, for the first time in his life,
under the spell of a woman: he is deeply affected by the sight
of Lesbia, Rhodope's hand-maiden. Kandaules notices this and
feels both amused and superior that Gyges should be captivated
by a girl whose beauty is really insignificant when compared
with that of Rhodope. The thought quickly becomes an obses-
sion with the King, who insists, now that the ring makes it possible, that Gyges must see for himself how far the beauty of
Rhodope exceeds that of all other women. Gyges understands
that what Kandaules requires of him is wrong, but his moral
sense is numbed by the quickening of his curiosity and desires
at the sight of Lesbia, and he succumbs to the powerful impulse
to come closer to the mystery of woman.

The consequences are immediate and catastrophic. Gyges,
invisible in the royal bed-chamber, no sooner sees the Queen
than he is stricken by a sudden awareness of the enormity of his
deed, an awareness which is made perfect by the love for her
which is instantaneously kindled in his heart. A sigh of remorse
escapes him, and he deliberately twists the ring upon his finger
so that in a flash his image comes and goes, leaving Rhodope uncertain what she has heard and seen, but sure that some kind
of desecration has been attempted. At first she feels that she
must pay with her life for her defilement, but Kandaules is able
to allay her fears and persuade her that nothing of moment has
occurred during the night. But then, eager to assure her that

he has gained in love and tenderness for her, tells her that he will be able to be more attentive than he has been recently, because Gyges will shortly leave the court.

This news crystallizes the vague doubts and suspicions in Rhodope's mind. She is convinced that it was Gyges whom she saw in that brief flash during the night, and that guilty fear is now driving him away. With this she undergoes a radical change. Whereas at first she was a passive figure, more or less like Genoveva, Agnes Bernauer, or even Klara, all of whom suffered tragedy merely by virtue of being differentiated from the Whole, at this point she becomes an active figure, another Mariamne, imperiously demanding the recognition of her rights. In a way, the change she undergoes resembles the change which takes place in the character of Kriemhild in the *Nibelungen,* a change from the loving and submissive woman to the implacable avenger. With the recognition that in some imperfectly understood way Gyges was the intruder, she bends every thought and every effort of the will to achieving vengeance. When she demands of Kandaules that he put Gyges to death and he gives evasive answers, she feels that this puzzling behavior is not merely incomprehensible, but that it threatens her sanity. She then resolves to command her faithful servant Karna, who has come with her from her native land, to intercept Gyges and bring him before her so that she may compel Kandaules to make the choice between slaying him and seeing her kill herself.

Gyges appears before Rhodope, trembling. When Rhodope accuses him of trembling because he knows what his guilt is, he frames a reply which reveals his love and veneration for her, while attributing his feelings to Kandaules: "Erinn're dich der Stunde, wo er dir/ Zum ersten Mal ins Antlitz schauen durfte,/ Und frag' dich, ob er mir nicht völlig glich." (Remember the hour when he was for the first time permitted to look upon your countenance, and ask yourself whether he did not completely resemble me). And as he goes on, out of his imagination recreating Rhodope's first encounter with Kandaules until he comes to the secret which is the husband's alone, how he wooed and won her: "Nun weisst du denn, warum ich zitterte:/ Ein Wonneschauer war's, der mich ergriff,/ Ein heil'ges Grausen, das mich schüttelte,/ Als ich so plötzlich vor dir stand und sah,/ Dass Aphrodite eine Schwester hat." (Now you know why I trembled:

it was a shudder of ecstasy which seized me, religious awe that shook me as I stood so suddenly before you and saw that Aphrodite has a sister). Although deeply disturbed and moved by Gyges' words, she continues to insist that he must die, and he declares himself ready to accept her sentence of doom and adds that he would, indeed, already have taken his own life had Kandaules not prevented it.

At this moment Kandaules enters. Gyges tries to take all the blame upon himself, pleading that he knows nothing of the nature of women, and that his act was like that of a little boy who crushes a bright bird in his hands when he attempts to stroke it. Kandaules, however, will not accept the sacrifice that Gyges wishes to make for him and declares that it is he who is guilty. Thereupon he leaves, requesting Gyges to speak for him. And Gyges does so, comparing his friend to a priest who wished to kindle in another's heart the flame which blazes in his own heart to the glory of his God. But Rhodope feels only that Kandaules has surrendered his conjugal rights to Gyges, who is therefore now her husband save in name, and whose duty it is to kill the King. When Gyges protests that he cannot attempt to take his friend's life, Rhodope gives him the choice of that or having her kill herself; but if he does kill Kandaules, she will become his wife. So fierce is her thirst for vengeance that she would prefer Gyges to murder Kandaules rather than challenge him to a fair fight. Gyges, however, will not consent to this, and so they make the pact that she will await the outcome of the duel at the altar, ready to give Gyges her hand if he returns, ready to stab herself if Kandaules wins. Her final words to him betray that she has been touched by his love: "Du hättest mich der Heimat nicht entführt,/ Um so an mir zu tun!" (You would not have taken me from home to do me such a wrong).

Gyges, therefore, seeks out the King and challenges him to a life-and-death struggle in order to save Rhodope. Kandaules immediately replies that, since it is Rhodope's wish, he will give up his life at once, but Gyges will not accept Kandaules' self-sacrifice, saying that he came to fight on equal terms. Kandaules replies that even if he were to win, he could still take his own life. And so the two friends, who now love and admire each other more than ever, are compelled each to seek the other's life. Both, in their readiness to die, have anticipated death in the essentials, and Kandaules has attained an altogether new insight into his relation to the Whole. He speaks of this to Gyges before the combat and acknowledges that by using the ring for mere personal ends, he has challenged awesome, mystic forces, the very existence of which he would formerly have denied. One must not always ask what a thing is, he says, but sometimes also what it is held to be. Veils, crowns, rusty swords, none of these things have eternal value, but they are symbols of what the world (i.e. universal forces) has achieved in the last struggle. The unquestioning, unknowing adherence of the world to the outward forms of transcendent principles gives it health and strength in a refreshing sleep. And if the world clings in its sleep to the veils, crowns, and rusty swords, then woe to the intruder who would take these things away, for if he has not the strength of Heracles to effect radical change, the sleeping world will brush him aside and crush him as though he were some ineffectual insect.

Thus ripe for death, Kandaules falls in the ensuing duel, and Gyges returns to Rhodope, who with her maidens awaits him at the altar of Hestia. Thoas, who has informed the Lydians of what has happened, brings Gyges the crown on their behalf, and at the same time tells him that he must prepare to defend it at once, for the enemy across the border, encouraged by Kandaules' pacific rule, have broken the peace. Gyges, out of respect for his slain friend, wishes to postpone the marriage until he has subdued the invaders, but Rhodope insists that the ceremony be performed at once. Gyges consents to this but vows to go to meet the enemy immediately. Rhodope replies that she has also taken a vow. Gyges, in turn, reminds her of his love for her and his hope that it will be requited. At the altar of Hestia Rhodope then elevates the new-made King to be her consort. This done, she enjoins him to keep his vow as she is about to keep hers. And then, with the words: "Ich bin entsühnt,/ Denn keiner sah mich mehr, als dem es ziemte,/ Jetzt aber scheide ich mich so von dir!" (I am cleansed, for none has seen me save one who had the right. But now I part myself from you—thus), she stabs herself.

Hebbel wrote in a letter to Friedrich von Uechtritz (December 14, 1859) that his original interest in *Gyges und sein Ring* came from the story, and that the more universal aspect of what he was writing did not dawn upon him until he had completed it. But then, to his surprise, suddenly there emerged from the play the idea which dominated and unified it, the idea of *Sitte*, a word which may be glossed as morality, custom, usage, propriety, but for which it is extremely difficult to find a satisfactory English translation.

If we take *Sitte* as the dominating idea of the play, it is easy to see that, of the three main characters, only Kandaules is in revolt against it, and even he is only a half-hearted opponent. His attempts at reform are sporadic and superficial. His tragic experience stems mostly from his lack of reverence for the individual as imbedded in traditional moral faith. His rationalist's skepticism of transcendent values, his inability to respect what he does not understand, makes him take upon himself the primeval guilt of sex. It is the sin of many of Hebbel's manly characters and the sin of Hebbel himself. The conventional morality which Kandaules flouts is the defense of woman against desecration by man. As the individual challenging the Idea, Kandaules necessarily goes down to defeat. But in his defeat there is a reconciliation with the universal force, for he has arrived at an understanding of his relation to the Idea.

But Gyges also goes down to defeat, even though he is fully identified with the conservative and ethical forces, so that, for example, he has ready sympathy for the feelings of Thoas when Kandaules demands the new regalia. Gyges fails at only one point, and that is when he yields to Kandaules' wishes in the matter of Rhodope. Even then he feels that what he is about to do is wrong, but has no inkling of what he will later feel to be the enormity of his act. And thus a relatively minor transgression becomes fatal and brings upon him a tragic experience as great as that which befalls Kandaules and Rhodope. From the moment he sees Rhodope he knows that everything which life has to offer him already has passed into the possession of someone else. That the someone else is his best friend, that he must kill the friend in an effort to save Rhodope, and that the effort is vain, all this shows us Gyges, through whose agency the universal power triumphs, as the most tragic figure in the play.

Unless, indeed, this figure be Rhodope, but not merely because her chastity was violated by her husband and the one man who might have been her true love. To begin with,

Rhodope was, like Genoveva, sinless, in perfect accord with her gods, i.e., God or the Idea, and hardly differentiated from the world which produced her. Through the violation of her chastity, she feels estranged from that world and becomes obsessed with the determination to close the breach between herself and the universal power by atoning for her sin of individuation through death, which she awaits from Kandaules. But when Kandaules can neither have her killed because she is defiled, nor punish Gyges because he is the defiler, her determination to take vengeance for what has happened to her becomes fanatical, and she altogether loses contact with her gods in her drive to be again at one with them. Moreover, she feels love for the man whose gaze has defiled her, and thus she has become, if only by inclination, unfaithful to her husband. To her original sin of mere existence—the universal and general sin—has therefore been added a personal sin, which is only intensified by her attempt to cleanse herself through taking her own life. In doing this she becomes unfaithful to Gyges as well as to Kandaules, and we witness the outward denial of self in her voluntary death, a self-affirmation no less fierce than that of Mariamne.

CHAPTER 10

Literary Fame and Social Acceptance

SHORTLY after the completion of *Gyges und sein Ring*, Hebbel received the news of Elise Lensing's death on November 18, 1854; and about the same time he heard of Amalia Schoppe's departure for the United States. He had by this time acquired such serenity from his artistic, social, and domestic achievements that the thought of these two women no longer had the power to disturb him. About Elise he felt, as we have seen, that he would not, in the life to come, encounter anyone more readily. And as for Dr. Schoppe, he freely acknowledged his indebtedness to her and even wrote her a friendly note or two before her death on September 25, 1858. His diary for 1856 closes with an elegiac couplet expressing his prayerful thanks to the gods for having given him so much, and imploring them not to bestow further gifts, which could only frighten him; now he needs nothing but their protection. The high point of his domestic happiness was marked by the purchase of a modest cottage in Gmunden on Lake Traunsee in August, 1855. He commented on this purchase in his diary on August 14: "I have always considered Shakespeare beyond my reach, and I never imagined that I could approach him in any respect. But still, in my earlier years I would sooner have hoped to portray some character or depict a situation as he did, than I would have hoped to resemble him by buying real estate."

The finest expression of his serenity and of his gratitude to Christine for having made possible its achievement, is a verse tale called *Mutter und Kind*. The idea went back to 1846, the year of Hebbel's marriage, when, on December 24, he wrote in his diary that it is only wedded life that makes a human being a complete person. Some time later (January 22, 1847), he jotted down the bare sketch of the idea concerning a rich and childless couple who made it possible for two poor lovers to marry in return for their promise to let them adopt their first baby. As soon as the child is born, however, the young mother refuses to give it up.

In this truly idyllic creation, there is none of the pessimistic bitterness which characterizes Hebbel's dramas, be they tragedy or comedy. Even Hebbel's *idée fixe*, the universal dualism, does not intrude. This does not mean, however, that the poem is without dramatic tension and that it tells a uniformly happy story. The very subject matter precludes a carefree tale of good people who are free from suffering. There is unhappiness and grief; but it is most remarkable that all the main characters are noble and good, and that their nobility and goodness are enhanced by their experience.

Poverty has not demeaned the character of Christian and Magdalena, the hard working young people whose desire to marry is thwarted by their lack of means. Great wealth has not corrupted the merchant and his wife, whose desire for a child has not been realized. The merchant's wife is perhaps the most complicated and least admirable of the four. Her yearning for a child has become so intense as to exceed the normal: anything which even remotely suggests the thought of children can cause her to experience a fit of extreme depression. Hence, her husband's only care seems to be to find ways to distract her: as he says to his friend, the doctor, he could wish to be Catholic in order to make pilgrimages with his wife to the various shrines in the hope of a miraculous cure of her barrenness.

Despite the merchant's steadfast love and ever renewed attempts to please his wife, she has on many occasions allowed her disappointment to cast a shadow over their relations, a failing which she bitterly regrets when she has a vivid dream that her husband has died. The merchant is almost pure kindness and generosity. His first care is for his wife, but he has accepted their childlessness as a sign that he should try to alleviate the misery of the poor as far as is within his power. When his friend, the doctor, suggests that the wife's great longing can be fulfilled if the merchant will enable Christian and Magdalena to marry on the condition that they turn over for adoption their first-born child, the merchant agrees in order to please his wife. She accepts the suggestion avidly but she wishes to pass the child off as her own, for it is very important to her that the gossipy neighbors and friends be ignorant of the truth, i.e., that she has not been able to bear a child. Magdalena accepts the proposal because it makes it possible for her and Christian to marry. The only alternative is what Christian has decided he must do, to seek his fortune in the Californian goldfields. Magdalena has a horror of this idea because of the dangers to which Christian will be exposed. She dreads the probability that he will not return. Christian has misgivings and doubts about the merchant's plan, but his deep love for Magdalena prevails over his prudence.

And so the merchant's wife goes to Italy to await the birth of Magdalena and Christian's child. And the young couple are established on a good-sized farm, far from their native Dithmarschen, with all the things they need to insure their future prosperity. The plan is that, after Magdalena has weaned the baby, the merchant and his wife will call for the child on their way back to Hamburg, thus managing to pass the baby off as their own so far as the inquisitive neighbors are concerned. But Magdalena and Christian, who have experienced the greatest joy of their lives in caring for the child, grow sadder as the day approaches. Magdalena wishes to keep the child and flee, but Christian will not consent because he has given his word. Magdalena then runs away with the child, but Christian soon finds where she is hiding and now agrees that they cannot go through with the bargain. They put the house and possessions into the best possible order; Christian draws up a financial statement, paying himself and Magdalena the lowest current wages for their work on the farm, and the little family succeed in hiding from the merchant and his wife when they arrive. They then set out on foot to take a ship for America as their last desperate recourse, and manage to make their way past the various searchers who have been employed by the merchant to find them—not to arrest and punish them, however, or even to claim the child, for the childless wife has gained an insight into what she had demanded of Magdalena.

This the young couple learns from former acquaintances. When Christian hears that his honor has been called into question because of his attempt to flee the country, he goes with his family directly to the merchant's home. The wife, having been, as she says, purified in the fire of her anxiety for the missing couple and their child, rejoices that they have been found. And so, as in a fairy-tale, Christian and Magdalena are confirmed in their ownership of the farm. They have their child; and the merchant's wife, her sense of values restored, agrees with her husband that the poor must take the place of children in their lives but that Magdalena's child will have an especial place in her affection.

Mutter und Kind turned out to be, along with *Die Nibelungen,* Hebbel's most successful work, popular with the reading public and acclaimed by the critics. For it Hebbel was awarded a prize of two hundred Taler by the Tiedge Foundation for the best verse tale in the manner of Goethe's *Hermann und Dorothea.* Although it has not remained as high in the estimation of literary historians as Goethe's poem, it is a very considerable artistic achievement. The relaxed flow of the narrative, the smooth and easy hexameters, the sympathetic characters who live through crises of moral decision, the optimistic outlook, all these things bear testimony to the sure hand with which Hebbel shaped his material.

For Hebbel, the time from the autumn of 1856 to the end of 1860 was filled with great activity, both creative and social. Even while writing *Mutter und Kind,* he was at work on his most ambitious project, *Die Nibelungen,* his serious interest in which went back to the autumn of 1855. On February 18, 1857, he finished that portion of the drama which became the first two parts, *Der gehörnte Siegfried* and *Siegfrieds Tod. Mutter und Kind* was finished a scant month later on March 20. Because of the formalities connected with the award of the Tiedge Prize, and because of certain details connected with the publication of the poem, it did not appear in print until Christmas, 1858. After the completion of the verse tale, Hebbel turned to the task of preparing an edition of his collected poems. It appeared in September, 1857. Fall was usually his productive season, so it was understandable that after the poems were in print he turned again to dramatic composition. It is surprising that he did not try to finish the *Nibelungen* as quickly as possible, but instead turned to material from Russian history, the story of the false Dimitri, on which Schiller was working before his death. For Hebbel, too, the subject proved to be, so to speak, fatal: he died attempting to finish the play.

Some mention should also be made of his relation to other personalities of importance in the world of literature and culture. Klaus Groth, for example, also a native of Dithmarschen, but considerably younger than Hebbel, made a very favorable impression upon Hebbel by his poems, in which, for the first time, Low German dialect was used with truly poetical effect. Hebbel praised the work of his compatriot and did what he could to make it generally known throughout German-speaking lands. Uhland, as we know, had long been the object of his admiration and continued to be so. The collection of poems just mentioned was dedicated to him as the "first poet of the present day," a rather remarkable judgment when one recalls that Hebbel knew at least some of the work of Eduard Mörike and Annette von Droste-Hülshoff.[1] He was sufficiently impressed by Mörike's work to call upon him when he was passing through Stuttgart. On this occasion he seems to have had a genuine sympathetic insight into Mörike's unhappy situation (Mörike's home-life was wretched), for Mörike wrote in a letter to Emil Kuh[2] that Hebbel, contrary to expectation, did not seem at all brusque, ambitious and aggressive.

On another occasion, when Hebbel hoped to make a good impression upon a distinguished personality, he had poor success. This was when he was introduced to Arthur Schopenhauer by Wilhelm Jordan, a poet who attempted to modernize ancient Germanic and Classical myths and legends. At first the interview seemed to be going well as Schopenhauer praised *Maria Magdalene,* but after he had spoken appreciatively of the play, he suddenly asked Hebbel how he was able to provide such a good play with such a horrible preface. This question so discomfited Hebbel that it took him some time to recover and launch into a eulogy of Schopenhauer, who, out of perversity, chose to accept Hebbel's praise ironically. This was a terrible blow to Hebbel's pride, for he had, of course, anticipated talking with Schopenhauer on equal terms. He took pains to conceal his humiliation from everyone, even his wife, to whom he wrote on May 6, 1857: "I found [in Schopenhauer] a very jovial old gentleman, who said that he was comparable to a man who had lingered too long in the wings, and now that the curtain was rising, ran off, timid and abashed. . . . We would, if I lived in Frankfurt, unquestionably become friends. This time I merely wished to perform a duty, for to a man who began to write when I was born, I am the herald of posterity."

In May, 1858, the Grand Duke Karl Alexander of Sachsen-Weimar was visiting Vienna and expressed the wish to become acquainted with Hebbel. The Grand Duke informed Hebbel that the court theater in Weimar, where Dingelstedt was now director, was preparing *Genoveva* for presentation in about a month. Hebbel had already known of this from Dingelstedt, but now he received an invitation to be present at the performance. He arrived there on June 21, the day before the dress rehearsal, which he attended, and during which he was presented to Princess Karoline Sayn-Wittgenstein and her daughter Princess Marie. Princess Marie had read some of Hebbel's plays. They had made such an extraordinary impression upon her that she had conceived an overwhelming admiration for their author, which was only heightened by personal acquaintance, and the acquaintance ripened into lasting friendship sustained by an interchange of letters, mostly about literary and cultural matters. Some of Hebbel's letters were directed to the mother, Princess Karoline, who said that her personal acquaintance with him had been very pleasant and that he was not only a poet, but also witty and a man of the world.[3] No words of praise could have been more flattering to Hebbel, the brick-layer's son, except perhaps the words of Grand Duke Alexander, writing about Hebbel's *Die Nibelungen:* "I declare that after the works of Goethe and Schiller I know of no German work which approaches it. There is something of Michelangelo about that man."[4]

Hebbel had, therefore, attained what he most desired, literary fame and social acceptance, but the satisfaction of his ambition had not completely mellowed him. The old berserker fury could break out with terrible force. Thus on one occasion, when out walking with his intimate friend, Emil Kuh, he spoke of an enthusiastic letter he had just received from a young man who had been present the evening before at Hebbel's reading of *Gyges und sein Ring.* Hebbel observed that it was odd that the young man had not remained for the supper which followed, but had left hurriedly, saying that he did not feel well. Hebbel wondered whether he had not perhaps feigned his sudden illness in order not offend against his dietary laws. When Kuh confirmed that this was indeed the case, Hebbel flew into a rage.

[130]

"What," he cried, "the reason for his refusal to eat with us was really what I said as a joke, and what I could not consider possible! His stomach pains were only a sham and such an individual dares to cross my threshold and listen to me reading my fairest play! A fanatical Jew dares to expound his views of Greek myths and customs to me!"

Kuh's attempts to pacify Hebbel enraged him still more. "Dog," he shouted, "accursed dog. I had taken you for my equal, that is, a human being. But if you act the Jew against me by refusing to eat with me, then I will act the Christian against you! Then I will shout: 'Pariah! lick my boots clean, for I am the aristocrat and you are the menial! I sit at the gentlemen's table of civilization, and you sit at the servants' table of history.'" In order to calm Hebbel, Kuh, who was Jewish himself, had to point out that the passers-by assumed that Hebbel was abusing him by demanding that he lick his boots. This plea brought Hebbel back to his senses. He smiled, gave Kuh both his hands, and did his best to convince the curious spectators that he and Kuh were good friends.[5] The whole outburst was a remarkable bit of behavior for a man who numbered many Jews among his friends and intimate associates, and who felt that Jews were neither better nor worse than other human beings.

On the occasion just described, Emil Kuh acted with almost unbelievable self-denial out of love for the man whom he idolized. But eventually, as Kuh reports it, the demands Hebbel made upon him grew excessive. Hebbel insisted that even Kuh's fiancée must take second place. This demand proved to be too much. Kuh's ever repressed desire for independence of action and judgment broke out, and the two friends parted ways. The break with Kuh, which entailed also a break with his friend, Karl Debrois van Bruyck, caused Hebbel great bitterness and sorrow. He felt that Kuh had betrayed him, especially because only a few weeks earlier, when Karl Gutzkow had called Kuh a mere clerk, Hebbel had publicly denounced Gutzkow, thereby challenging this powerful figure to a literary feud. He was so shaken by the quarrel with Kuh, that, according to his own account, he could not sleep at night for two weeks. Nonetheless, he struggled mightily to complete *Die Nibelungen,* and was able to write in his diary on March 7, 1860, that he was just completing the fifth act of *Kriemhilds Rache,* the third and final part of his great trilogy.

CHAPTER 11

The Last Plays

I Die Nibelungen

DIE *Nibelungen,* often referred to as a trilogy, is perhaps more accurately described in Hebbel's own words as a "monster in eleven acts." That is, it consists of two five-act plays and a prologue in one act. It is a reworking in dramatic form of what has been justly called the greatest theme since Homer, the glory of Middle High German literature, the *Nibelungenlied.*

Hebbel first became acquainted with this titanic work in his Hamburg days when he came across a copy owned by Amalia Schoppe. Although at the time he did not read it in its entirety, it made a strong impression upon him which was renewed and immensely strengthened by the experience of seeing his wife act the part of Chriemhild in *Der Nibelungenhort,* a play by Ernst Raupach. Impatient with the cheap staginess of this play and the over-civilized treatment of the theme by Emanuel Geibel in his *Brunhild,* to say nothing of the precious sublimity of the earlier treatment by Friedrich de la Motte-Fouqué in his *Der Held des Nordens,* Hebbel was stimulated by one of the essays in Friedrich Theodor Vischer's *Kritische Gänge.* In this essay, Vischer suggested that the *Nibelungenlied* could not be put on the stage as a spoken drama, but would have to be set to music in order for justice to be done to the taciturn but emotionally charged characters. Needless to say, Richard Wagner did attempt something of this sort, although it can scarcely be said that his characters are taciturn. The effect which the essay had on Hebbel was to deter him from attempting to compose a spoken drama on the subject until he had attained a certain maturity.

Unlike Wagner, Hebbel drew only very lightly upon the Norse myths and legends. He was, on the whole, faithful to his main source, although, of course, he had to modify it in various respects in order to concentrate the action and elaborate the characterization of certain personages, notably Dietrich von Bern and Etzel. He also found it necessary to inject some mythologizing of his own in keeping with his mystical view of history. Whether these additions redound to the benefit of the work is at least debatable.

The age which is reflected in the *Nibelungenlied,* so Hebbel believed, was an age of historical crisis, the time of final settlement, in Europe, of the struggle between paganism and Christianity. This idea he expressed to Marie, Princess Wittgenstein, in a letter dated August 24, 1858: "I wish to represent how the two [the primitive Germanic and the Christian elements] gradually penetrate each other and create a new world." Three years later, on January 21, 1861 he wrote to Pastor L. W. Luck that his trilogy shows the triumph of Christianity over heathendom.

The myth which Hebbel devised to reflect his metaphysical view of history does not appear in its entirety in the final form of *Die Nibelungen,* but allusions to the whole structure are made by various characters, notably Brunhild's faithful servant Frigga, Brunhild herself, and Dietrich von Bern. In a passage which was later eliminated the myth is told by Dietrich von Bern. According to the myth, at the conclusion of each millennium there comes a moment in which a child of superhuman strength may be begotten, even by a weakling, for the child is heir to the strength of all nature. At such a time, the world, shaken to its depths, changes form. The past struggles out of its grave, the future strives to be born, and the present defends itself. When this occurs, the dead gods have the power to revive an infant girl who has died at the precise moment when the superhuman child was conceived. It is the purpose of the gods to marry these two to each other. If they succeed, a new race will be produced which will threaten the existence of mankind. The human race, however, in self-defense produces a woman of perfect beauty to rival the giantess. If the superman chooses the human bride, humanity is safe for another thousand years. The application to the characters and action of *Die Nibelungen* is plain: Siegfried, Brunhild, Frigga, and the Norse gods represent a primordial stage of historical evolution; most of the other characters, although nominally Christian, are heathen at heart and live by the absolute ethical norms of personal bravery, fealty, honor, and revenge. The inexorable duty to exact vengeance is, of course, the feature of heathendom which brings about its collapse. The chaplain, Rüdeger, and Dietrich von Bern represent the new form of the Idea, Christianity, with its ethical norms of self-control, humility, and readiness to forgive.

The prologue, *Der gehörnte Siegfried,* is a skillful combination of exposition and complicating action. Very quickly Hebbel puts his audience in possession of the essential information. We see the court of the Burgundian kings, Gunther, Gerenot, and Giselher, and their devoted follower, Hagen, the dominating figure at the court, whose Christian faith is only a thin veneer over his innermost paganism. The minstrel Volker, Hagen's friend, tells the court about Siegfried, the invulnerable slayer of the dragon, possessor of the Nibelung treasure and Alberich's cap of invisibility. All this is well known to Hagen, but he does not know of the fearsome maiden, Brunhild, who lives on savage Isenland, sworn to defend her maidenhood against every suitor, to wed only the man who can overcome her in combat but to slay everyone who fails. When Gunther, the eldest of the three kings, hears this tale, he is seized with an impetuous and foolish resolve to have Brunhild for his wife.

At this moment, Siegfried appears with twelve warriors to challenge the Burgundians to fight for their kingdom. Apprised of who the doughty challenger is, Gunther courteously declines to fight and offers Siegfried whatever he may wish to take. Siegfried, shamed by this gentle reception, modifies his challenge to a contest in weight-throwing and offers his friendship. He, of course, easily wins the contest, surpassing even Hagen. Then Siegfried reveals that his real purpose had been to ask for the hand of Kriemhild, sister of the Burgundian kings. Gunther readily agrees, but with the one reservation that Brunhild come to Worms as his Queen before Kriemhild have his sanction to marry.

Siegfried vainly tries to dissuade Gunther from this mad venture, for there is only one champion in the world who can overcome her, and that champion, Siegfried himself, will never choose her. But when Gunther persists, Siegfried suggests that there is one way for Gunther to win Brunhild and that is for Siegfried, made invisible by Alberich's cap, to do the actual feats while Gunther goes through the motions. When this strategy is accepted, Siegfried tells the story of how he slew the dragon and how he gained invulnerability, save for one spot where a leaf fell upon him as he bathed in the dragon's blood, the Nibelung treasure, and the peerless sword, Balmung. Armed with this sword, he went to seek out Brunhild and found access to her castle blocked by a lake of fire. When he swung the sword three times about his head, the flames died down, and he stood there, invisible in Alberich's cap, but able to see Brunhild. He was not drawn to her, however, and went his way without being known. Gunther repeats his wish for Siegfried to lead him to Isenland and win Brunhild. Volker cautions that it is unseemly to resort to unfair means, but his words are not heeded. Hagen, however, reminds them all, by putting his finger to his lips and striking his sword, that the affair must be kept a strict secret.

The second part of the drama, *Siegfrieds Tod,* opens in Brunhild's castle on Isenland. Odin, whose power has been repressed by Christian rites, has tried to communicate with Brunhild through Frigga, who feels that some disaster is about to overtake them. Gunther and his followers arrive to challenge Brunhild, and she accepts after she has had a vision in which she sees herself as a Valkyrie, made deathless. Preparations for the contests are made, Siegfried acting in every respect as Gunther's vassal. Siegfried's stratagem works, and Gunther seems to be the victor. Siegfried hastens back to Worms, acting as Gunther's messenger. He tells the good news and at the same time manages, although shyly and clumsily, to confess his love for Kriemhild. Kriemhild, who has been in love with Siegfried ever since she watched him in contest with her brothers and Hagen, cannot conceal her tenderness for him, and the prospects for happiness are fair. But when Gunther arrives with Brunhild and the others, Hagen approaches Siegfried to ask him for his help again, for Brunhild has refused to yield herself to Gunther, and Gunther's strength does not match hers. There is, therefore, only one solution. Siegfried must subdue Brunhild once again, but this time in the bridal chamber.

When out of fear for her life Brunhild has been brought to the point of swearing obedience and submission, Siegfried leaves Gunther to consummate the conquest which he has prepared. Unfortunately, however, Brunhild had tried in her nocturnal struggle with Siegfried to tie his hands with the jewelled girdle she wore. Siegfried took it from her and, to keep her from using it again, slipped it inside his shirt. The following morning Kriemhild finds it lying on the floor of their room and asks Siegfried for an explanation. Siegfried, completely honest and simple, is unable to keep the truth from his wife, who is thereby put into possession of a terrible weapon that might be used against Brunhild. And it is so used, but only under extreme provocation. Brunhild conceives a terrible hatred of Siegfried because she has hidden doubts of her husband's prowess. According to Frigga's prophecy, the owner of the sword Balmung should have come through the fiery lake to claim her, but instead the flames died down and no one came. She therefore constantly nags Gunther to show his superiority to Siegfried, something which, of course, he cannot do. It does not, therefore, take much for jealous and hateful words to be exchanged by Brunhild and her sister-in-law, Kriemhild. The latter, finally goaded beyond endurance, shows Brunhild the fateful girdle as proof that it was Siegfried, not Gunther, who subdued her. Brunhild, whose supernatural strength has vanished, now calls upon Gunther to avenge her upon Siegfried. Hagen, more jealous of his King's honor than the King himself, insists that Siegfried must be slain, and Gunther yields to his insistence. This means murder, for Siegfried is invulnerable except in one spot. Hagen is able to persuade Kriemhild to reveal the location of the vulnerable spot, on the pretext that only in this way can he protect Siegfried in battle. Once he knows the spot, it is easy for Hagen to trick Siegfried into laying aside his armor, thus exposing himself to the spear which Hagen hurls with deadly accuracy.

The third part of the drama, *Kriemhilds Rache,* covers the events of the second half of the *Nibelungenlied,* compressed and simplified to meet the needs of the drama. It begins with the embassy of Rüdeger von Bechlaren to King Gunther to sue on behalf of his liege lord, Etzel, King of the Huns, for the hand of Kriemhild. Kriemhild has passed the years in deep mourning for Siegfried, giving aid and comfort in her husband's name to the sick and needy, until Hagen, foreseeing that her generosity would raise an army to support her against himself and the Kings, took from her the treasure of the Nibelungen. Now when news of Etzel's proposal comes to her, she impatiently rejects it until she hears that Hagen is opposed to it. Then, after securing from Rüdeger an oath equally binding upon Etzel and himself that they will not deny her any service, no matter what it might be, she formally accepts the offer of marriage and is escorted to Etzel's capital, Vienna, by Rüdeger and his men. The Burgundians, however, do not accompany her, but promise to come to visit sometime in the future upon her invitation.

When that time comes, the Burgundians make the perilous journey, Hagen being certain that Kriemhild has summoned them to their death, but Gunther relying for protection on Kriemhild's love for her mother and for Giselher, her youngest brother, who, like Gerenot, had nothing to do with the murder of Siegfried. On the way, Hagen acts as guide and protector, slaying attackers and keeping all the Burgundians from harm. He is aided by Volker, to whom he confides his forebodings. When the Burgundians arrive at Rüdeger's castle in Bechlaren, they are given a cordial welcome. It is their last happy time. Rüdeger's wife, Götelind, gives Hagen a magnificent shield that belonged to her father. Volker notices that Giselher is drawn to Rüdeger's daughter, Gudrun, and brings about their betrothal. All approve the match, Volker and Hagen chiefly because they hope that Rüdeger will be their staunch ally at the court of Etzel. The hope is vain, however, for Kriemhild lives for only one thing, to bring about the death of Hagen, and will spare no one who opposes her in this aim.

Etzel, although he feels that he can refuse her no request whatsoever because she has borne him an heir, tries to keep the peace and commands that the banquet be held as planned. But while Hagen and the Kings are at the table, Kriemhild's followers, Huns whom she has won over in large numbers by promise of dividing the Nibelungen treasure among them as a reward for killing Hagen, attack the men under the command of Hagen's brother, Dankwart, and kill them all. Dankwart fights his way to the banquet hall and cries out to Hagen what has happened. At this moment, Etzel and Kriemhild's little son is being presented to the guests. Hagen seizes the boy and lops his head off. Dietrich von Bern and Etzel withdraw, Etzel to order a general battle against the Burgundians and Dietrich to bide his time. Wave after wave of Hunnish soldiers attack the Burgundians, who seem almost invincible, surviving even the burning of the banquet hall.

Finally the time comes when Kriemhild sends Rüdeger into combat against the kinsmen he had so recently gained and sworn alliance with. Rüdeger pleads to be released from his oath, but Kriemhild is inexorable in her demand that Hagen must be slain—the others she will let go. But they all refuse to deliver him up to save themselves, and Rüdeger must go to fight. After killing Gerenot and Giselher, he is killed by Hagen, who, together with Gunther, alone survives. Etzel dons armor to attack these two but is held back by Dietrich, who overcomes both survivors and brings them, bound, out into the open. Kriemhild now finds one mutilated Hunnish soldier to whom she must, according to the terms of her pledge, give the treasure of the Nibelungen. When she turns on Hagen and demands to know where he has hidden the hoard, he replies that he has vowed not to disclose the secret as long as any of the Kings might live. She sends the Hun to murder Gunther. When the Hun returns with Gunther's head, Hagen laughs in triumph, for now he alone knows where the treasure lies and he will never tell. Kriemhild, in a fury, tears the sword from the unresisting Hagen and kills him. At this, Dietrich von Bern's faithful follower, the ancient Hildebrant, can no longer endure that the instigator of so much killing should herself remain alive, and he kills Kriemhild. Etzel, overwhelmed, feels unequal to the task which his code now imposes upon him, to continue the never-ending chain of revenge killings. He turns to Dietrich, begging him to relieve him of his crown and bear the burden of the world upon his shoulders. Dietrich assents in the name of Him who died upon the cross.

On December 31, 1859, Hebbel, in the midst of his work on *Kriemhilds Rache*, wrote to the critic Hermann Hettner, explaining his conception and intention. Some passages from this letter are, perhaps, the best commentary on the work:

What gives me some confidence of success in my uncertain undertaking, even in my sober hours, is the circumstance that, in spite of the colossal dimensions of the characters, the motives of their actions are so infinitely simple, and, as the story progresses, result so naturally one from the other. Siegfried leaps out beyond the limits of nature, and scarcely knows what he is doing when he anoints himself with the dragon's blood and makes himself invulnerable. What can be simpler, since the opportunity which is suddenly offered him must be seized just as suddenly if it is not to be lost forever? But it is no less simple, either, that Hagen, the never-vanquished and never-humbled, who, under other circumstances, would surely never have avoided an honorable fight with him, should believe himself justified in resorting to a dishonorable fight because of his invulnerability which puts him on a plane with the elements. Actually, he does the very same thing Siegfried has done, only in another sphere and in a different way. In this I see the actual center of the tragic conflict and, I hope, with good reason, since the whole poem is wonderfully illuminated from this point out to the most distant radii—I am strongly inclined to prefix my play with these verses from the *Ajax* [of Sophocles] as a motto: "For enormous and inhuman bodies are always obnoxious to the Gods." In this way I would recall the aboriginal outlook of the Greeks and the coincidence of this view with the Germanic outlook laid down in this mighty epic. And that is exactly how it is with Kriemhild. Roused by Etzel's suit from her complete, unthinking, and actually dream-like passivity, which goes so far that not even her child, Siegfried's son, means anything to her, she grasps his hand, because the most powerful sword in the world flashed in it. She then tries to get Hagen in her power, for she does not doubt that her brothers, who, fearing his anger, did not prevent him from killing Siegfried, would not, from fear of Etzel, prevent her from taking revenge on him. The brother-in-law, the guest, was not safe under the protection of King Gunther. How could the vassal be safe, so safe that the King staked his person and life, his whole house, upon him? She miscalculates and must miscalculate, for Hagen is no superman, as Siegfried was. But the noblest victims fall even during her first endeavor: how could she stop before reaching a goal from which she would have recoiled in horror, if she had seen it clearly to begin with?

Hettner was, of course, not the only prominent literary figure with whom Hebbel corresponded about his *Nibelungen*. Franz Dingelstedt followed the progress of the composition with great interest and enthusiasm, and planned to have the drama performed in Weimar. Although Hebbel had some misgivings about the success of a performance in Weimar, where the resources, including the actors, were not all that could be desired for a major performance, he did assent to Dingelstedt's request. On January 31, 1861, *Der gehörnte Siegfried* and *Siegfrieds Tod* were performed with great success. The Grand Duke Karl Alexander of Sachsen-Weimar and his Duchess were even kinder to Hebbel than they had been during his previous visit to Weimar, not only honoring him as a distinguished public figure, but also admitting him into the most intimate circles. On two evenings, Hebbel read *Kriemhilds Rache* aloud. The Grand Duke was greatly impressed and expressed his hope that Hebbel would attend the Weimar performance of this part of the trilogy also. Dingelstedt set about arranging for such a performance. News of the effective production of the first two parts was ill received by the directorate of the Hofburg, which had already rejected them. Their displeasure increased when Christine Hebbel was invited to come to Weimar as a guest artist to perform in the trilogy, and, worse still, when she received leave through the intervention of the Grand Duke with the Emperor. The whole trilogy was successfully performed in Weimar on May 16 and 18, 1861.

While the Hebbels were in Weimar on this occasion, their dissatisfaction with conditions at the Hofburg under the directorship of Laube were, quite naturally, discussed. Dingelstedt proposed that they come to Weimar where Christine could become a regular member of the Weimar theater. The Grand Duke and the Duchess added their pleas, and for a while it seemed very possible that the move would be made. But a change of atmosphere had taken place in Vienna because of the great success of *Die Nibelungen* and the widespread interest in the play. And a change of atmosphere took place in Weimar also. Apparently Dingelstedt began to fear that the Hebbels would rise altogether too high in the favor of Karl Alexander, and he began to talk about the disadvantageous aspects of being attached to the Weimar theater. Hebbel made inquiries of various experienced people concerning conditions in Weimar and

[140]

was warned against going there. Since in addition Hebbel had misgivings about living in such a small city, nothing came of the proposed change.

Still further time was required, however, for the Hofburgtheater to attempt a performance of *Die Nibelungen.* But, finally, on February 18, 1863, ten months before Hebbel's death, the first two parts were given with great success.

II   Demetrius

The few years that were left to Hebbel after the completion of *Die Nibelungen* were largely dedicated to other things than creative writing. In October, 1861, he went to Berlin and Hamburg to conclude negotiations about the publication of *Die Nibelungen.* On this occasion he paid a visit to his brother, of which more will be said later. At about the same time, he was engaged in a polemic against Friedrich Bodenstedt, whose book on Shakespeare's contemporaries Hebbel had unfavorably reviewed.

These polemical articles did not arouse nearly as much interest and excitement as did a poem addressed to "His Majesty, King Wilhelm I of Prussia." The occasion for the poem was the attempt on the life of the King by a young man named Oskar Becker. Hebbel was dismayed and enraged by an attack on the representative of the State, that is, the Idea, asking how it was possible for anyone thus to invite the repression of liberal tendencies. He implored the King to consider that his life had been spared in order to allow him to accomplish great things, such as the unification of Germany and the establishment of the welfare of his subjects. In the poem he pointed to dangers threatening not only German lands but also the Austrian Empire, for, he said, the menial nations, the Czechs and the Polacks *[sic]*, were shaking the ancient structure. No sooner had this poem been published than the newspapers and journals of the Slavic populations heaped abuse upon Hebbel. But after a few months the tempest died down, whether or not it was true, as Hebbel said, that the Bohemians and the Poles began to hurl the epithet of menial nation at each other in forgetfulness of its original use.

In February, 1862, Hebbel was officially asked to compose the "Prologue" to the celebration of the first anniversary of the adoption of the Austrian constitution. A year later, to his chagrin, he discovered that three other poets, men for whose work he had scant respect, had already refused the honor. In May and June of 1862, Hebbel visited England, especially London, in the company of a Hofrat Marshall, a native Englishman and secretary to the Grand Duchess of Weimar. Back on the continent, he received an invitation from the Grand Duchess to come to her summer residence, Wilhelmsthal, where he had already passed some delightful days.

In a way, this visit to Wilhelmsthal represents the high point of Hebbel's life, the perfect fulfillment of his early craving for the social recognition which he had now attained through his literary achievement. It was a brief rest, a time of mellow reflection, before the swift decline and death. A fellow guest at Wilhelmsthal, the critic and connoisseur, Adolf Schöll, has left an interesting account of the impression Hebbel made upon him and the other guests. Schöll arrived at Wilhelmsthal after Hebbel had been there for a few days and found him,

free of the feeling of not being accustomed to the social circle which he had entered with some diffidence. The sense of being at ease, which the Duchess knows how to impart unnoticed to her guests in a delicate and perceptive consideration of each one's idiosyncrasies, was reflected in the cheerful equanimity of his mood. That which talents that have attracted general attention are apt to take for granted, when they are admitted into the most distinguished society, namely to allow all facets of their brilliantly endowed personalities to glitter, did not in any way accord with Hebbel's disposition. And as soon as he had perceived that the Duchess had not the least intention of having him perform in her salon, but wished only to express her high esteem of his accomplishments and her kind feelings for him personally, he reveled in soothing ease. Of all the various artists and writers who, for years, had occasionally been guests of the court, none to the same degree as Hebbel had restricted himself in conversation to polite attentiveness and courteous deference, without ever giving, to say nothing of seeking, an occasion for a witty remark, story, or monopoly of the conversation. This, however, was not taciturnity, but deliberate surrender to the recreation devotedly offered him; it was natural, easy participation in this gently moving small circle of elegant society, and natural assimilation to the enjoyment of the charms of nature offered by the palace buildings and the paths through the park in the midst of the forest. The regimen gave the desire of the guest time and scope enough for resting or strolling in voluntary solitude or easily found company, to enjoy pure refreshment of the spirit, and in such moments I had a feeling of warmth and well-being at his side.[1]

How far our poet had risen in his life's journey is strikingly illustrated by a passage from Hebbel's letter to Christine of October 19, 1861, during the trip to Hamburg which has already been mentioned. In this letter, Hebbel describes a visit to his brother, who was living in almost exactly the same circumstances as their father before his death, the same circumstances from which Mohr had rescued him.

Hebbel had a little difficulty in finding his brother, who had moved to a different locality.

But [he says] I found the right village, which is situated on this side of a small grove of trees; and a plowman pointed out the house to me. When I walked around the corner, I caught sight of an oldish man, who was chopping wood outside his door. A weatherbeaten face, still framed by abundant hair, looked up at me, puzzled, as I approached, still in some doubt but nonetheless quickly discovering the lineaments of youth in the lines and wrinkles, I stretched out my hand and said "Johann!" in Low German, of course. He dropped his axe, slapped his knees, ran his hand through his hair, broke out into convulsive laughter; in short, did everything that I am accustomed to do in a moment of sad and happy surprise, and it was impossible to calm him. Shaking his head and rubbing his hands, he then led me inside. I walked through a small kitchen into a living room, which, so far as space and furnishings went, was no worse, perhaps somewhat better than what our parents had. His wife, a peasant woman, like our housekeeper in Gmunden, apologized for the general disarray, but, she explained, it wasn't Sunday until tomorrow. She was much more relaxed and offered to make coffee, an offer which I would not have refused for anything in the world, although I knew what kind of a chicory brew awaited me. Little Conrad was not at home, he was going for bread. The cat, which is always to be found in such families, lay on the bed. Titi's wooden cuckoo stood on the chest. My brother began to whistle on it. The coffee was brought in, and it was not entirely undrinkable. There was fresh goat milk for it, which was obtained from two goats that belong to him and which I later went to visit in their little stall. The neighbors' children gathered and looked inquisitively in through the window, while the grown-ups came to their door ways. Finally the child came, too, a good-looking,

[143]

blond lad, with large clear, bright eyes. He was timid, like a bird, and could scarcely be induced to come closer by the offer of a silver Taler. He slipped away again at once and now looked in from outside also. My brother disappeared too, and when I looked around for him, I found him in the kitchen, shaving and trimming his hair. You see, I had asked him to go with me back to Rendsburg, and he said that he was really too shaggy. In his haste he cut himself three times with his dull razor, and he stanched the cuts with blotting paper. After about an hour and a half we set out on the road back, he in the old Styrian coat I sent him in the spring, with a shapeless summer hat on his head and on his feet rough shoes that scarcely held together. Bitter poverty: a little heap of potatoes under the stove and a domestic dispute as to whether more potatoes or wood and peat should be bought for the next cash. My brother was for the potatoes, his wife for the fuel. "I fear hunger," he said, "and she fears cold." You can imagine that I settled the dispute.—In Rendsburg I had to call on one of his friends. At first I refused to do so, because I did not understand the reason and he said nothing more. Then I asked, "Would it mean a great deal to you?" and he answered, "Yes, yes, he will find out anyhow that you were here and he helps me out at times."—In my inn I ordered something to eat. He livened up considerably over a glass of beer— but otherwise he is terribly run-down and he has a very convulsive manner.—He no longer eats meat, only potatoes.—When I was packing, he asked me for one of my silk handkerchiefs that was torn. I asked, "I suppose you want to take it along to the old woman?" He replied, "That too, of course, but it is more because of the people! I will tell them, 'That is the poorest one he had.' "

The year 1863, the year of Hebbel's death, began for him both auspiciously and inauspiciously. As we know, his *Nibelungen* was given on February 19 for the first time in Vienna and was a fine success. And his birthday, March 18, was observed both far and near. The Libertas student association held a *Kommers* in his honor, and he received telegrams and presents from everywhere. Undoubtedly what he most prized was the gift of a silver goblet from the Grand Duchess of Sachsen-Weimar and the title of Private Librarian to the Court of Weimar conferred upon him by the Grand Duke. Unfortunately, however, an illness which had long been latent broke out a few days before his birthday, so that he was confined to bed. During his remaining months his condition varied, sometimes seeming hopeful, at other times discouraging. And then, strange to say, about

October 11, his vein of poetry began to flow once more, and he resumed work on the play which he had begun in 1857, *Demetrius*.

Although the actual composition of *Demetrius* did not start until 1857, when Hebbel had to interrupt his work on *Die Nibelungen* because of his sudden intense interest in the Russian theme, the idea for a play about a prince who is ignorant of his paternity had been with him for a long time, perhaps ever since his seventeenth year, as he asserted in a letter to Moritz Kolbenheyer.[2] From a diary entry we know that he was turning the idea over in his mind around March 19, 1838. At this time, however, it seemed to him to be a good subject for a comedy. Three years later, in the diary entry for January 21, 1841, he writes of the dilemma in which such a prince would find himself: his every decision would be wrong. The next diary entry which is concerned with the subject (February 10, 1849) omits all mention of the comic possibilities and sketches this situation: a prince who has been brought up in ignorance of who he is, commits a murder, but just as the law is about to exact the penalty, it is revealed that he is above the law. This is basically what happens in the prologue of the play as we now have it.

From the foregoing brief account of the stages of development through which Hebbel's conception of the unknown prince passed, it can readily be seen that the theme had special significance for him, that he probably identified himself with Demetrius, and that the sufferings which Demetrius endured from being essentially far above his menial position are a reflection of the young Christian Friedrich in the service of Kirchspielvogt Mohr, a reflection, that is, as the mature Hebbel presented it to himself and us.

The situation of the young Demetrius is, in a word, intolerable. He is, without knowing it, the illegitimate son of Ivan the Terrible and a palace serving woman named Barbara. He has been placed in the household of the *voivod* or governor of Sendomir in Catholic Poland by the Jesuits, who hope to use him to open up the Russian Empire to the Roman Church. To this end they believe they have persuaded Barbara to steal the infant son of Ivan and Marfa, the Empress, and replace him by her own son, born at the same time. Thus the true heir to the throne would receive a Catholic upbringing. Fortune seems to favor their plot when the presumed young prince comes to a violent end, having been murdered, according to rumor, by order of the usurper, Boris Godunow. Barbara, however, has deceived the Jesuits, for it was her own and Ivan's son she turned over to them. With the death of the real prince, therefore, there comes to an end the line of Russian rulers whose legitimate descent from Rurik constitutes their absolute right to the throne.

The illegitimate child of Ivan, as he grows up in Sendomir, comes to the point where he can no longer endure his position of being half-menial, half foster-son of Mniczek, the *voivod*, and in love with Mniczek's daughter, Marina. He has a natural majesty, an inborn power to command respect, an overwhelming sense of being superior to all the servants of the household and even to his master and the Polish nobles who come to visit him. Thus his very being is illegitimate, for he is forbidden every natural expression of his feelings. His situation has become so unbearable that, when the opportunity presents itself, he attempts a kind of suicide. This comes about when he is rebuked by the nobleman, Odowalski, for being too familiar with Marina. In a fury Demetrius challenges Odowalski, who naturally refuses to fight a man of doubtful social status. Thereupon Demetrius attacks and kills him, fully expecting to be put to death for the murder. But instead, the monk Gregori and the Cardinal-Legate come forward with the proclamation that Demetrius is the heir to the throne of Russia and therefore above the law. For the first time in his life Demetrius feels that he has the right to be his true self, but he has won this right by means of a murder, and, more than that, by a murder which constitutes a challenge to the social order. His guilt is more than the mere guilt of existence. Although from the beginning he upholds the principle of legitimacy and manifests scrupulous regard for law, he cannot recall the challenge to the Idea and has condemned himself at the outset.

The struggle for power which Demetrius undertakes is, from the first, a struggle for acknowledged legitimacy. To the end of securing the recognition and the blessing of the Empress Marfa for Demetrius as her true son, the Empress is taken against her will from the convent, where she has found peace, to confront the new pretender to the throne. Demetrius succeeds in convincing her that it was contrary to his wishes and commands that she had been forcibly brought before him. Finally she consents to show herself in his company to the army, thereby allying herself with his cause, but she has not attained the intuitional certainty she needs in order to confirm that Demetrius is her son. She resolves to go to Moscow to pray at the tomb of the murdered child. There she feels that certainty will come.

Her visit to Moscow coincides with the triumphal entry of Demetrius into his capital. As he rides past the tumultuous crowd, an old woman, seeking to touch his cloak, slips and falls at his feet. He lifts her up, and, as compensation for the injury she has received in falling, he asks her to come to see him the next day. The old woman, of course, is his mother, Barbara, unknown to him. Meanwhile, the Empress Marfa has come to the mortuary chapel of the line of Rurik, and she kneels in prayer by the murdered boy's tomb, shedding tears of compassion and repentance for her own sins. Demetrius' enemies point out to the populace that Marfa's tears make it seem doubtful that she believes in the legitimacy of the new Czar. While this is being discussed, Mniczek arrives and orders the coffin of the child to be removed from the chapel, where it has no right to be. Marfa implores him to leave the coffin where it was. Despite Mniczek's urging that she must give orders to have the coffin removed if she is not to bring ruin upon Demetrius, she is unable to give the command: she has attained intuitional certainty that the murdered child, not Demetrius, is her son. Nonetheless, when Demetrius asks her blessing, she gives it gladly, saying, "Be happy as you are great and noble," not, "as you are the true Czar."

Meanwhile, the number of Demetrius' enemies has increased, for various selfish interests have been disappointed by his respect for law and justice. A revolutionary conspiracy has been formed, headed by Prince Schuiskoi, who has ambitions to become Czar himself. Mniczek, the realist and practical man of action, does his best to counter the revolution by arresting Schuiskoi and persuading Demetrius to sign the warrant for his execution. To add to the difficulties, the monk Gregori appears and explains the role of the Roman Church in seating Demetrius on the throne. He points out that Demetrius can pay his debt to the church by admitting the Jesuit order into Russia. Demetrius refuses, saying that this is a matter which concerns the Patriarch of Moscow, not solely the Czar. In the midst of this conversation, Barbara appears at the time appointed by Demetrius, who has learned from Gregori half the truth of her role in the Jesuit's scheme. Demetrius, at first suspecting that Barbara must be vile and mercenary, gradually is convinced of her good character. Then, since he has before him the woman who really knows, he asks her whether he is not the son of Ivan. When Barbara affirms that she can take the most sacred oath that he is, Demetrius asks her to go with him to the Empress to persuade her that he is Marfa's son. This, of course, Barbara cannot do, and so the secret is revealed and Demetrius understands that he is, indeed, the son of Ivan, but illegitimate.

His first impulse is to give up his power immediately and set Prince Schuiskoi free to become his successor, and to call the nobles together, reveal the truth, and seek their leave to return to Poland, where the executioner will be waiting for him. Mniczek, however, is quick to point out that this course of action will mean the abandonment and death of himself, his daughter Marina, and all of Demetrius' devoted followers. Demetrius is therefore compelled to go on acting the part of Czar until the safety of his dependents is ensured. "I am captain of a foundering ship," he says. "Quickly into the life boat with you, and then I'll light the powder magazine."

Just how the play would have been worked out, if Hebbel had finished it, is impossible to say. The fourth act ends with the words just quoted, and of the fifth act he wrote only two hundred and thirty-one lines. The remaining action would necessarily have been swift. Demetrius would probably have been murdered by order of Schuiskoi, whom he had pardoned, and the murder would probably have taken place at the moment of his highest moral triumph.

Thus, even though Demetrius has taken personal guilt upon himself in the murder of Odowalski, his death is an expiation not only of personal guilt, but equally, or even more so, of the metaphysical guilt of individuation. In Hebbel's universe every individual is illegitimate. Demetrius is doubly so—essentially and existentially. He is like the unsuspecting prince mentioned in the diary: whatever course of action he takes will be wrong. He is so tormented by the restraint put upon him by his situation and by the denial of his right to be himself, that he prefers death to life and takes guilt upon himself. Could he have avoided guilt at this time, it would have been only through the sacrifice of his individuality, a death in life. But the life which is opened up to him is just as illegitimate and doomed to failure, as the old one, because Demetrius, as he has shown by his every action since he took on the role of Czar, reveres established tradition and believes in the principle of legitimacy. Although he is in his mind and soul at one with the prevailing form of the Idea, as an individual he is necessarily illegitimate and must go down in defeat in his struggle with the Adversary.

The ability to work on his play was undoubtedly, next to the love and devotion of his family, Hebbel's greatest consolation during his illness, for it seemed to promise the recovery for which he yearned. Beginning in October, he wrote until the brink of death, when he could no longer control his pencil. In that time he wrote nearly two acts of what, had he completed it, might have been his finest play. On November 10, news reached him from Berlin that he had been awarded the Schiller Prize. Smiling wistfully, he remarked: "This is human destiny: at some times there is no wine, at others no goblet." Of even greater significance to him was undoubtedly the reconciliation with his most loyal and devoted friend, Emil Kuh, who appeared one day as though his daily visits had never been interrupted. To the last he maintained his intellectual interests, dictated letters to his correspondents, kept up with contemporary events, and listened to his wife and daughter read to him from the classics. On December 13, 1863, at twenty minutes past five in the morning, he died quietly. He was carried to his final resting place by representatives of the student organizations. Despite the pouring rain, a large crowd attended.

CHAPTER 12

Conclusion: Hebbel's Contribution to German Drama

IN conclusion a few words concerning Hebbel's position in German and European literature may be in order. It can safely be said that Hebbel brought at least two things to German drama: revelation of the motives of his characters more penetrating and analytical than had ever been attempted, and a conception of historical determinism, such as we have seen, for example, in *Herodes und Mariamne*.

If we call to mind some of the most memorable character creations of Hebbel's great predecessors and contemporaries, it soon becomes apparent that no playwright before him had presented to his hearers or readers such a deep-delving exposition of the process of character development that resulted in precisely such and such and no other personality.

The presentation of character development was apparently a task that had escaped the other dramatists. What we have of this kind of exposition in Lessing's Nathan or Tellheim can scarcely be called such. And if we go to the most memorable dramatic characters conceived between the creative periods of Lessing and Hebbel, to Goethe's Gretchen, who is more vitally alive than almost any flesh and blood human being that treads the earth, to Schiller's Wallenstein, whose fault may well be both in his stars and in himself that he is a failure, to Heinrich von Kleist's Elector of Brandenburg, who seems to pardon the young Prince von Homburg from new and different motives of his own each time the play is read or performed, to Grillparzer's mighty Ottokar, king of kings, who caused his own works to crumble into dust, in no case do we learn why and how the characters have become what they are, as we do in Hebbel's plays through becoming acquainted with the pre-history of the characters.

Conclusion

Goethe, to be sure, invented a background and a pre-history for Gretchen, as, indeed, he did for Shakespeare's Hamlet, but Gretchen's pre-history found its place in *Die Leiden des jungen Werthers*—Goethe's pre-history of Hamlet, incidentally, found its place in *Wilhelm Meisters Lehrjahre*. Klara's pre-history in Hebbel's *Maria Magdalene*, however, is part of the warp and woof of the play, the action of which moves forward through revelation of the past. This technique, the so-called analytic exposition, is at least as old as Sophocles' *Oedipus Rex*, and was used to fine comic effect by Heinrich von Kleist in his *Der zerbrochene Krug* a little before Hebbel. But with Hebbel it became a standard part of his dramatic strategy, a strategy which was later employed, though not so rigorously, by Ibsen in such plays as *Pillars of Society* and *Ghosts*, and by Gerhart Hauptmann in *Das Friedensfest* and *Vor Sonnenaufgang*, for example.

As for historical determinism, this Hegelian idea had not found expression in the drama before Hebbel. To be sure, there had been a good many plays based on significant historical episodes or personages, Goethe's *Götz von Berlichingen* for one, most of Schiller's plays, quite a few by Kleist, Grillparzer, and others. Schiller in his *Maria Stuart*, for example, made no attempt to construct the play so that the action would flow inevitably from the historical situation in which the rival queens, Mary Stuart and Elizabeth I, found themselves. Their struggle does not necessarily and specifically proceed from the historical situation of the British Isles and Europe in the second half of the sixteenth century as Schiller understood that situation. For Schiller, the historical placement of their struggle was something of an accident, the essential thing being the tragic spectacle of human ennoblement through an act of moral will, an act which can be performed by any potentially noble human being anywhere at any time. "*Verteufelt human*," devilishly humanistic, was Goethe's word for such an outlook in his own case. But in *Herodes und Mariamne*, as we have seen, the great chess game between Herod and the Adversary in the guise which Hebbel postulated that He or It assumed in Judea in the pre-dawn of the Christian era, has already been played almost to its conclusion. Only two identical moves are left to Herod to save the situation: he must throw away so as not to lose. But Herod, being who he is at the time and in the place he is—not actually the Judea of history, of course, but the golden realm of Hebbel's thought—cannot do what he is required to do to beat the Adversary, and he becomes the tragic victim of history.

Hebbel was not content, however, to leave it all at that, but felt that his drama must offer not merely a philosophical exposition of times of historical crisis, but also a criticism of contemporary problems. In *Maria Magdalene, Julia,* and *Ein Trauerspiel in Sizilien* he attempted direct criticism of some of the evils of his age as he saw them. Of the three plays only the first is successful; and it is, of course, this play which causes Hebbel to be put down as a forerunner of modern realistic drama, a kind of German Ibsen, who may have anticipated in a tentative, rather old-fashioned way the work of the much better known and more influential Norwegian.

That Ibsen's plays have some things in common with Hebbel's is obviously true, the most striking feature probably being the use of analytic exposition, as we see it, for example, in *Ghosts,* where the mental collapse of Oswald is shown to be a natural consequence of the prevailing social conditions and moral standards. Ibsen can be linked with Hebbel through *Ghosts* in another way, and that is the concern with the morbid and fatal effects of extreme dissipation which we have seen in Hebbel's *Julia.* And Ibsen's *The Lady from the Sea* can be looked upon as a dramatized amplification of Hebbel's maxim, "*Wirf weg, damit du nicht verlierst,*" "Throw away so as not to lose."

It is also sometimes stated that Ibsen's women owe much to Hebbel's Rhodope, and that Nora is a more modern Mariamne. And here, of course, is where the case for a true affinity between the works of Ibsen and Hebbel breaks down. The absurdity of the proposition becomes apparent if it is remembered that Nora, preparing to dance the tarantella, teases Dr. Rank by showing him her flesh-colored tights.

It becomes immediately apparent how far apart from Ibsen Hebbel really is if we try to imagine Mariamne showing her flesh-colored tights to the Roman Titus. The idea is ridiculous, if not shocking, and its impossibility is a very great tribute to the intense earnestness of Hebbel, as well as to his ability to endow character with independent life. Nora is anything but a more modern and highly developed Mariamne, and Hebbel is certainly no tame prefiguration of Ibsen, whose intellectual forebears can sooner be found among Hebbel's contemporaries and foes, the Young Germans, with their insistence that the function of the writer is to help in bringing about social reform.

Ibsen, with often comic irascibility, castigates the pillars of society in the apparent hope of revealing them and thus rendering them less harmful. As a satirist he has a practical aim. Hebbel, however, is basically neither a satirist nor a reformer, and he rejects the notion that social betterment either can or should be the aim and function of art, for it is through art that the individual comes to an understanding of his relationship to the Whole, of his mysterious separation from and revolt against it, and of his inevitable tragic reconciliation with it. The two playwrights, regardless of many superficial points of resemblance —more than can be counted up here—are philosophically and artistically very far apart indeed, and it is doubtful that Hebbel would ever have acknowledged Ibsen as his spiritual descendant.

Notes and References

Chapter One

1. See Paul Bornstein, *Hebbels Persönlichkeit*, II, 28-31 and 39-40.
2. See Friedrich Hebbel, *Briefe*, ed. R. M. Werner, VIII, 2.
3. See Bornstein, I, 596-97.
4. See the essays on Hebbel in Wolfgang Liepe's *Beiträge zur Literatur- und Geistesgeschichte*. To Liepe goes the distinction of having demonstrated the links between Hebbel's thought and the philosophy of his day.

Chapter Two

1. See Wolfgang Liepe, "Hebbel und Schelling," in *Beiträge zur Literatur- und Geistesgeschichte*, pp. 218-19.

Chapter Three

1. See Hebbel, *Briefe*, II, 90 and 91, esp. 91, lines 10 and 11. Hebbel had apparently kept up a correspondence with Beppi Schwarz and informed Elise about it.

Chapter Four

1. Bernt von Heiseler, in his essay "Versuch über Hebbel" in the collection *Ahnung und Aussage*, suggests that Hebbel, in learning standard High German, cut himself off from the rhythms and melodies of his native Low German; hence a certain formalistic stiffness in his language. This suggestion may go a long way towards explaining the lack of naturalness in his humor.

Chapter Five

1. The "feel" of the play is predominantly North German, but there are South German elements in it also. Anton has traits which Hebbel had observed in his father; and the Secretary, whose name is Friedrich, shares certain traits with Hebbel. Meister Anton got his name, however, from Anton Schwarz, the cabinet-maker in whose home Hebbel lived for a while in Munich. Beppi Schwarz

is, of course, the original of Klara: on one occasion, as has been noted, she told Hebbel how she had been seduced by an unworthy man. Hebbel's reaction was that of the Secretary in the play: inability to repress a bitter feeling. As a consequence, Beppi came close to committing suicide.

2. For a discussion of the lower-middle-class attitude toward pre-marital relations, see R. M. Werner's introduction to the play in Hebbel *Werke*, II, xviii-xiv.

3. Grillparzer could never feel comfortable in Hebbel's presence. "I am actually afraid of him," he is quoted as saying. "He is too clever for me—he often introduces such curious topics of conversation. For example, he is capable of asking, 'What is God?' Well, I don't know, but he does, and then, you see, I have nothing to say." Bornstein, II, 277.

4. Emil Kuh, *Biographie Friedrich Hebbels*, II, 167.

5. Bamberg, when editing Hebbel's selected correspondence, destroyed Hebbel's letters to Elise written during the winter of 1845-46. For this reason it is necessary, at this point, to resort to conjecture.

6. Elise Lensing, *Briefe an Friedrich und Christine Hebbel*, ed. Rudolf Kardel, pp. 145-46.

7. *Ibid.*, p. 60.

Chapter Six

1. Emil Kuh, II, 233.

Chapter Seven

1. Such admirers were, besides Kuh, Emil Rousseau, Wilhelm von Zerboni, and Sigmund Engländer. Rousseau, as we know, died very young. Zerboni, who is mentioned quite infrequently in Hebbel's diaries and letters, was overtaken by financial disaster which he himself invoked by extravagant living. The last reference to him in the diaries is dated December 22, 1849: "Yesterday I had the pleasure of taking thirty-two florins to Zerboni for his essays in the *Reichs-zeitung*. Now he will have what he needs for the holidays after all." Hebbel broke with Engländer because of the latter's political radicalism. When Kuh began to entertain thoughts of marriage and devoted to his bride-to-be time to which Hebbel felt he had exclusive claim, their ways parted. Hebbel, of course, maintained that the fault lay entirely with Kuh. They were reconciled on Hebbel's death-bed. The friendship with Engländer was restored in 1862, when Hebbel was traveling in England, and Engländer, who had settled in London, acted as his guide.

2. Bornstein, I, 354.

3. Bornstein, I, 238.

Chapter Ten

1. Annette von Droste-Hülshoff was no longer alive—she had died in 1848—but Hebbel had become acquainted with her poems by 1845. On January 16 of that year, he wrote in a letter to Felix Bamberg: "It is disagreeable to me that the *Allgemeine Zeitung,* which is the only one read abroad, still ignores me, as if I were less important than Annette von Hülshofen *[sic],* from whom a reviewer recently dated a new epoch of literature." If Hebbel ever over-estimated himself as a poet, he surely did so on this occasion.
2. Kuh, II, 426.
3. Bornstein, II, 16.
4. Bornstein, II, 144.
5. Kuh, II, 463.

Chapter Eleven

1. Bornstein, II, 207-08.
2. Br. VI, 244.

Selected Bibliography

PRIMARY SOURCES

HEBBEL, CHRISTIAN FRIEDRICH. *Sämtliche Werke.* Historisch-kritische Ausgabe besorgt von R. M. Werner. Berlin, 1901 ff. Erste Abteilung: *Werke.* 12 vols. Zweite Abteilung: *Tagebücher.* 4 vols. Dritte Abteilung: *Briefe.* 8 vols. The standard edition of Hebbel's works.

————. *Sämtliche Werke.* ed. H. KRUMM. 12 vols. Hamburg, 1891-92.

————. *Werke,* ed. GERHARD FRICKE, WERNER KELLER, and KARL PÖRNBACHER. Munich, 1963-. The most recent comprehensive edition. Still in process of publication.

Neue Hebbel-Dokumente, ed. DIETRICH KRALIK and FRITZ LEMMERMAYER. Berlin and Leipzig, 1913.

Hebbel-Dokumente. Unveröffentlichtes aus dem Nachlass, ed. R. KARDEL. Heide, 1931.

Neue Hebbel-Briefe, ed. ANNI MEETZ. Neumünster, 1963.

LENSING, ELISE. *Briefe an Friedrich und Christine Hebbel,* ed. R. KARDEL. Berlin and Leipzig, 1928.

SECONDARY SOURCES

BARTELS, ADOLF. *C. F. Hebbel.* Leipzig, 1899.

————. *Hebbels Herkunft und andere Hebbel-Fragen.* Berlin and Leipzig, 1921.

————. *Friedrich Hebbel und die Juden.* Munich, 1922.

BIACH, ADOLF. *Friedrich Hebbel und die Juden.* Brüx, 1897.

BIEBAU, GUSTAV. "Der Kirchspielvogt Mohr," *Hebbel-Jahrbuch* 1965. (Heide in Holstein, 1965), pp. 165-77.

BLAUSTEIN, LEOPOLD. *Das Gotteserlebnis in Hebbels Dramen.* Berlin, 1929.

BORNSTEIN, PAUL. *Friedrich Hebbels Persönlichkeit.* 2 vols. Berlin, 1924. Indispensable for an understanding of Hebbel the man.

BRUN, LOUIS. *Hebbel. Mit besonderer Berücksichtigung seiner Persönlichkeit und seiner Lyrik.* Leipzig, 1922.

BRUNS, FRIEDRICH. *Friedrich Hebbel und Otto Ludwig: Ein Vergleich ihrer Ansichten über das Drama.* Berlin-Steglitz, 1913.

CAMPBELL, T. M. *The Life and Works of Friedrich Hebbel.* Boston, 1919. Noteworthy for its compact, yet elegant style and sensitive literary judgment.

――――. "History as Costume in Hebbel's Drama." *MLN*, XLI (1926), 489-95.

――――. "Hebbel's *Herodes und Mariamne*, 11.1289-95," *MLN*, XLIV (1929), 250-53.

――――. *German Plays of the Nineteenth Century.* New York, 1930, pp. 16-19, 212-314.

CASTLE, EDWARD. "Der falsche Demetrius in der Auffassung Schillers und Hebbels," *Jahrbuch des freien deutschen Hochstifts*, 1930, pp. 232-56.

DIEBOLD, EDMUND. *Friedrich Hebbel und die zeitgenössische Beurteilung seines Schaffens.* Berlin and Leipzig, 1928.

DOSENHEIMER, ELISE. *Das zentrale Problem in der Tragödie Friedrich Hebbels.* Halle, 1925. An exposition of the view that the man-woman problem is central in Hebbel's plays.

FLYGT, S. G. *Friedrich Hebbel's Conception of Movement in the Absolute and in History.* University of North Carolina Studies in the Germanic Languages and Literatures, No. 7. Chapel Hill, 1952.

――――. "Revelation-Scenes in the Plays of Friedrich Hebbel," *GR*, XXVIII (1953), 23-33.

FRENKEL, J. *Friedrich Hebbels Verhältnis zur Religion.* Berlin, 1907.

FRISCH, HELGA. *Symbolik und Tragik in Hebbels Dramen.* Bonn, 1961.

GANSBERG, MARIE LOUISE. "Zur Sprache in Hebbels Dramen," *Hebbel in neuer Sicht*, ed. HELMUT KREUZER. (Stuttgart, 1963), pp. 59-79.

GEORGY, E. A. *Das Tragische bei Friedrich Hebbel.* Leipzig, 1922.

――――. *Die Tragödie Hebbels nach ihrem Ideengehalt.* Leipzig, 1911.

GRAHAM, P. G. *The Relation of Drama to History in the Works of Friedrich Hebbel.* Smith College Studies in Modern Languages, XV, Nos. 1-2, 1933-34.

――――. "The Principle of Necessity in Hebbel's Theory of Tragedy," *GR*, XV (1940), 258-62.

HECHT, WOLFGANG. "Hebbels *Diamant*," *Hebbel in neuer Sicht*, ed. HELMUT KREUZER. (Stuttgart, 1963), pp. 208-27.

HEISELER, BERNT VON. "Versuch über Hebbel," in *Ahnung und Aussage* (Munich, 1939), pp. 81-91.

Selected Bibliography

HENEL, HEINRICH. "Realismus und Tragik in Hebbels Dramen," *PMLA*, LIII, 502-518.

HERMAND, JOST. "Hebbels *Nibelungen*—ein deutsches Trauerspiel," *Hebbel in neuer Sicht*, ed. HELMUT KREUZER. (Stuttgart, 1963), pp. 315-333.

HEWETT-THAYER, H. W. "Ludwig Tieck and Hebbel's Tragedy of Beauty," *GR*, XI (1927), 16-25.

ISAACS, EDITH J. R. "Concerning the author of *Herod and Mariamne*," *Theatre Arts Monthly*, XXII (1938), 886-90. Testimony to the interest in the ill-fated American production starring Katherine Cornell, in November, 1938.

JANSSEN, ALBRECHT. *Die Frauen rings um Hebbel*. Berlin and Leipzig, 1919.

JOKISCH, W. "Hebbel-Literatur, 1919-30," *Archiv*, 163, (1933), pp. 34ff.

KREUZER, HELMUT, ed. *Hebbel in neuer Sicht*. Stuttgart, 1963. A collection of essays presenting some of the most recent points of view.

KREUZER, HELMUT. "Hebbels *Gyges und sein Ring* (im Rahmen der Stoffgeschichte)," *ibid.*, (Stuttgart, 1963), pp. 294-314.

_____. "Hebbels *Agnes Bernauer* (und andere Dramen der Staatsraison und des politischen Notstandsmordes)," *ibid.*, pp. 267-93.

KREUZER, INGRID. "Hebbel als Novelist," *ibid.*, pp. 150-63.

KRUMM, J. *Die Tragödie Hebbels, ihre Stellung und Bedeutung in der Entwicklung des Dramas*. Hebbel-Forschungen, III, Berlin, 1908.

KUH, EMIL. *Hebbel*. Wien, 1877. Third ed., 1912. Still the indispensable biography, although inadequate and even wrong in some respects.

LIEPE, WOLFGANG. "Der Schlüssel zum Weltbild Hebbels: Gotthilf Heinrich Schubert." *Beiträge zur Literatur- und Geistesgeschichte*. Neumünster, 1963, pp. 139-57. Most important. This and the other studies by Liepe made untenable certain long-accepted ideas about Hebbel's relation to contemporary thought.

_____. "Hebbel zwischen G. H. Schubert und L. Feuerbach. Studien zur Enstehung seines Weltbildes." *Ibid.*, pp. 158-92.

_____. "Hebbel und Schelling." *Ibid.*, pp. 193-258.

_____. "Unbekannte und unerkannte Frühprosen Hebbels. Untersuchungen zur ersten geistigen Entwicklung des Dichters." *Ibid.*, pp. 259-303.

_____. "Hebbels philosophisches Jugendmärchen 'Die einsamen Kinder.'" *Ibid.*, pp. 304-29.

――. "Hebbels Tagebuchpräambel und ihr Ideenhintergrund." *Ibid.*, pp. 330-43.

――. "Zum Problem der Schuld bei Hebbel." *Ibid.*, pp. 362-81.

――. "Friedrich Hebbel: Weltbild und Dichtung." *Ibid.*, pp. 382-98.

LUKACZ, GEORG VON. "Zur Soziologie des modernen Dramas," *Archiv für Sozialwissenschaft und Politik,* XXXVIII (1914), 303-345, 662-706.

MARCUSE, LUDWIG. "Der Hegelianer Friedrich Hebbel—gegen Hegel," *Monatshefte,* XXXIX (1947), 506-14.

MARTINI, FRITZ. "Der Lyriker Hebbel. Theorie und Gedicht," *Hebbel in neuer Sicht,* ed. HELMUT KREUZER (Stuttgart, 1963), pp. 123-49.

MEETZ, ANNI. *Friedrich Hebbel.* Stuttgart, 1962. A succinct summary of essentials, with a quick review of the present state of Hebbel studies.

MEYER-BENFEY, H. *Judith.* Göttingen, 1913.

――. *Hebbels "Agnes Bernauer."* Weimar, 1931.

MICHELSEN, PETER. *"Beitrag zu einer Hebbel-Bibliographie,"* *Hebbel-Jahrbuch,* 1953, pp. 111-33. Continued irregularly with contributions by others in the *Hebbel-Jahrbuch.*

――. "Friedrich Hebbels Tagebücher. Eine Analyse ihrer weltanschaulichen Grundgehalte." Diss. Göttingen, 1951.

――. "Das Paradoxe als Grundstruktur Hebbelschen Denkens," *Hebbel in neuer Sicht,* ed. Helmut Kreuzer (Stuttgart, 1963), pp. 80-108.

MÜLLER, JOACHIM. *Das Weltbild Friedrich Hebbels.* Halle (Saale), 1965. An attempt to make Hebbel out to be something of a Marxist.

――. "Zur Struktur und Funktion von Hebbels Tagebüchern," *Hebbel in neuer Sicht,* ed. HELMUT KREUZER (Stuttgart, 1963), pp. 109-22.

NAUMANN, WALTER. "Hebbels *Gyges und sein Ring."* *Monatshefte,* XLIII, (1951), 253-70.

PFANNMÜLLER, GUSTAV. *Die Religion Friedrich Hebbels auf Grund der Werke, Tagebücher und Briefe dargestellt.* Göttingen, 1922.

PFEIFFER, F. L. "The Moral Problem in Hebbel's Drama," *GR,* II (1927), 148-56.

PLACZEK, HEINZ WALTER. "Das historische Drama zur Zeit Hebbels." Diss. Munich, 1927.

POPPE, THEODOR. "Hebbel und sein Drama," *Palaestra,* VIII (1900).

PURDIE, EDNA. *Friedrich Hebbel. A Study of His Life and Work.* London, 1932.

Selected Bibliography

RYAN, LAWRENCE. "Hebbels *Herodes und Mariamne,*" *Hebbel in neuer Sicht,* ed. HELMUT KREUZER (Stuttgart, 1963), pp. 247-66.

SCHAPIRE-NEURATH, ANNA. *Friedrich Hebbel.* Leipzig, 1909.

SCHEUNERT, A. *Der Pantragismus als System der Weltanschauung und Aesthetik Hebbels.* Second ed., Leipzig, 1930. Very influential, but now generally considered too rigid and extreme in its formulation.

SCHOLZ, WILHELM VON. *Hebbel. Das Drama an der Wende der Zeit.* Stuttgart and Berlin, 1922.

SCHUELER, H. "Hebbel's Poetic Use of the Dream," *GQ,* XIV (1941), pp. 1-17.

SHEPARD, F. L. "Hebbel's *Gedanken-Lasten* in the *Maria Magdalene,*" *JEGP,* XXX (1951), pp. 80-86.

SOMMERFELD, MARTIN. *Hebbel und Goethe.* Bonn, 1923.

STERN, MARTIN. "Das zentrale Symbol in Hebbels *Maria Magdalene,*" *Hebbel in neuer Sicht,* ed. HELMUT KREUZER (Stuttgart, 1963), pp. 228-46.

SULGER-GEBING, EMIL. "Die Uraufführung der *Agnes Bernauer* am Münchener Hoftheater," *Euphorion,* XX (1913), pp. 121-41.

TIBAL, ANDRÉ. *Hebbel, sa vie et ses œuvres de 1813 à 1845.* Paris, 1911. A masterful presentation, very rich.

WAETZOLDT, WILHELM. "Hebbel und die Philosophie seiner Zeit." Diss. Berlin, 1903.

WAGNER, A. M. *Hebbels Drama, eine Stilbetrachtung des Dichters und seiner Kunst.* Hamburg, 1911.

WALZEL, O. *Hebbelprobleme.* Leipzig, 1909.

———. *Hebbel und seine Dramen.* Leipzig and Berlin, 1927.

———. "Vom Wesen des Tragischen," *Euphorion,* XXXIV (1933), pp. 1-37.

WERNER, H. "Der konservative Staatsbegriff in Hebbels Dramen," *Grenzboten,* LXXII, pp. 532-34.

WERNER, R. M. *Hebbel. Ein Lebensbild.* Berlin, 1913.

WIESE, BENNO VON. *Die deutsche Tragödie von Lessing bis Hebbel.* 2 vols. Hamburg, 1948. II, 334-461.

———. "Die Religion Büchners und Hebbels," *Hebbel in neuer Sicht,* ed. HELMUT KREUZER (Stuttgart, 1963), pp. 26-41.

———. "Das Tragische in Hebbels Welt- und Kunstanschauung," *Euphorion,* XLI (1941), pp. 1-21.

WINTERFELD, ACHIM VON. *Friedrich Hebbel. Sein Leben und seine Werke.* Dresden, 1908.

WITTKOWSKI, WOLFGANG. "Der junge Hebbel. Zur Entstehung und zum Wesen der Tragödie Hebbels." Diss. Frankfurt, 1955.

――――. "Hebbels *Genoveva,*" *Hebbel in neuer Sicht,* ed. HELMUT KREUZER. (Stuttgart, 1963), pp. 185-207.

――――. "Hebbels *Judith,*" *ibid.,* pp. 164-84.

WOLFF, HANS M. "Die Doppelstellung Herzog Albrechts in Hebbels *Agnes Bernauer,*" *Monatshefte,* XXXI (1939), p. 209.

WOLFF, HANS M. and LUDWIG MARCUSE. "Noch einmal: Hebbel und Hegel," *Monatshefte,* XL (1948), pp. 157-60.

WRIGHT, J. D. "Hebbel's Klara: The Victim of a Division in Allegiance and Purpose," *Monatshefte,* XXXVIII (1946), pp. 304-16.

WÜTSCHKE, H. *Hebbel-Bibliographie.* Berlin, 1910.

ZIEGLER, KLAUS. *Mensch und Welt in der Tragödie Friedrich Hebbels.* Berlin, 1938. An attempt to judge Hebbel's plays independently of his theories and comments on them.

――――. "Wandlungen des Tragischen," *Hebbel in neuer Sicht,* ed. HELMUT KREUZER (Stuttgart, 1963), pp. 11-25.

ZIEGLSCHMID, A. J. F. *Beiträge zu Friedrich Hebbels Charakterkunde. Ein psychologischer Deutungsversuch.* Berlin, 1932.

ZINKERNAGEL, F. *Die Grundlagen der Hebbelschen Tragödie.* Berlin, 1904.

Index

Index

Elvers, Paul, 21

Elvers, Wiebke, 21

Employment: Hebbel's father and, 13, 16; as parish clerk, 17-21, 145; Amalie Schoppe and, 23-24, 39-40; as Weimar Court Librarian, 144

Enghaus, Christine, see Hebbel, Christine Enghaus

England, 68, 142, 156n1

Engländer, Sigmund, 156n1

Ense, Karl August Varnhagen von, 106

Erlangen, University of, 76

Ernst, Duke of München-Bayern (as character), 107-15

Etzel (character), 133, 137-38, 139

Europa (periodical), 58

Evil, see Guilt

Faust (Goethe), 68, 76

Ferdinand, Emperor of Austria, 91

Feuchtersleben, Ernst von, 116

Feuerbach, Ludwig, 22

France, Hebbel in, 63, 65, 66, 67, 76, 77

Frankfurt, Hesse: Schopenhauer in, 129

Frankfurt Parliament, 99

Franz Karl, Archduke of Austria, 91

Freihafen (periodical), 101

French, 66, 77

Friedensfest, Das (Hauptmann), 151

Friedrich (character), 71-72, 73, 74, 75; Hebbel and, 35, 82-83, 155-56

Friendship: with women, 21-22, 26-27, 34, 49, 82; with Rousseau, 28-29, 35-36; Vienna circle, 102-103, 156n1; in *Gyges und sein Ring*, 118, 121-22, 123; *anti-Semitism* and, 130-31. See also individual names.

Frigga (character), 133, 134, 135, 136

Fürth, Bavaria, 38

Gartner, Franz, 36

Gehörnte Siegfried, Der (Hebbel), 128, 134-135, 140

Geibel, Emanuel, 132

Genevieve, Saint, 49

Genoveva (Hebbel), 41, 49-55, 56, 75, 79; publication of, 59; *Agnes Bernauer* and, 107, 110, 114; operatic setting for, 116; *Gyges und sein Ring* and, 120, 124; Weimar production, 130

German, 129, 143, 155

Germany: nationalism and, 32, 99, 103, 141; drama of, 150-53. See also specific place-names

Gervinus, G. G., 116

Ghosts (Ibsen), 151, 152

Glaser, Julius, 102

Gmunden, Austria, 125

God, 26, 32-33, 42-43; the individual and, 45-47, 51, 53, 54-55, 64-65, 75. See also Idea, The

Goethe, Johann Wolfgang von, 13, 25, 29, 76, 130; Strassburg and, 30; Napoleon and, 60; Tieck and, 106; Tiedge Prize and, 128; characterization and, 150, 151

Golo (character), 49, 50-52, 53, 55, 110

Golo und Genoveva (Müller), 50

Görres, Joseph, 35

Gotha, Saxe-Coburg-Gotha, 38

Göttingen, Saxony, 38-39

Index

Index

on Emma Schröder, 48; on comedy, 56; on etiquette, 60, 62, 80-81; on sentimentality, 67; on middle class values, 75; tion, 122-23; on *Die Nibelungen*, 133, 138-39, 140; on Johann Hebbel, 143-44; on *Demetrius*, 145

Levetzau, Marshal, 60

Libertas association, 144

Liepe, Wolfgang, 22-23, 155

Literature: in Hebbel's childhood, 14, 16; Mohr and, 19, 20; early influences, 22-23; Heidelberg and, 28, 29; Munich and, 31; political, 32, 103, 112-15, 116, 153, historical necessity and, 54; Scandinavian, 61, 63-63; plastic arts and, 77; achievements of Hebbel, 150-53. *See also specific forms, i.e.,* Drama; Novellas; Poetry

London, England, 142

Love, *see* Friendship; Sex

Low German dialect, 129, 143, 155

Luck, L. W., 133

Ludwig I, King of Bavaria, 114-15

Ludwig, Duke of Ingolstadt-Bayern (as character), 108, 109, 110, 111

Maler, Friedrich, *see* Müller, Friedrich

Maria Magdalene (Hebbel), 35, 63, 69-79, 79; foreword, 65, 66, 67-69, 74, 129; dedication, 78; Christine Enghaus and, 82-83; in Leipzig, 87; *Julia* and, 88, 89, 90; in Vienna, 99;

passivity of Klara in, 120; character development in, 151, 155-56; social criticism in, 152

Mariamne (character), 92-95, 96-98; Rhodope and, 120, 124, 152

Maria Stuart (Schiller), 151

Marie, Princess of Wittgenstein, 130, 133

Marshall, Hofrat, 142

Mary, Queen of Scotland (Schiller character), 151

Maximilian II, King of Bavaria, 114-15

"Maximilian Friedrich Hebbel an seine Mutter" (Hebbel), 67

"Mein Wort über das Drama" (Hebbel), 63, 64-65

Meissner, Alfred, 102-103

Meta, 14

Meyr, Melchior, 114

Michel Angelo (Hebbel), 104-105

Michelangelo Buonarroti, 77, 104-105, 130

Middle class, 68-69; morality and, 69-76, 82-83, 89, 156

Mohammedanism, 54

Mohr, J. J., 17-21, 85, 143, 145

Mohr, Otto, 17-18

Moloch (Hebbel), 104

Moltke, Helmuth von, 59, 60

Montez, Maria (Lola), 114

Morality: historical imperative in, 68; middle-class, 69-76, 82-83, 89, 156; decadence and, 90, 152; religion and, 104, 105, 134; tradition and, 122, 123

Mörike, Eduard, 129

Motte-Fouqué, Friedrich de la, 132

Mozart, Wolfgang Amadeus, 36

DATE DUE

GAYLORD			PRINTED IN U.S.A.